T0316681

Cambridge Elements ≡

Elements in Psychology and Culture
edited by
Kenneth Keith
University of San Diego

THE NATURE AND CHALLENGES OF INDIGENOUS PSYCHOLOGIES

Carl Martin Allwood
University of Gothenburg, Sweden

CAMBRIDGE
UNIVERSITY PRESS

CAMBRIDGE
UNIVERSITY PRESS

University Printing House, Cambridge CB2 8BS, United Kingdom

One Liberty Plaza, 20th Floor, New York, NY 10006, USA

477 Williamstown Road, Port Melbourne, VIC 3207, Australia

314–321, 3rd Floor, Plot 3, Splendor Forum, Jasola District Centre,
New Delhi – 110025, India

79 Anson Road, #06–04/06, Singapore 079906

Cambridge University Press is part of the University of Cambridge.

It furthers the University's mission by disseminating knowledge in the pursuit of
education, learning, and research at the highest international levels of excellence.

www.cambridge.org
Information on this title: www.cambridge.org/9781108461689
DOI: 10.1017/9781108562171

First published 2018

A catalogue record for this publication is available from the British Library.

ISBN 978-1-108-46168-9 Paperback
ISSN 2515-3986 (online)
ISSN 2515-3943 (print)

The Nature and Challenges of Indigenous Psychologies

DOI: 10.1017/9781108562171
First published online: August 2018

Carl Martin Allwood
University of Gothenburg, Sweden

Abstract: The indigenous psychologies (Ips) stress the importance of research being grounded in the conditions and culture of the researcher's own society due to the dominance of Western culture in mainstream psychology. The nature and challenges of Ips are discussed from the perspectives of *science studies* and *anthropology of knowledge* (the study of human understanding in its social context). The Element describes general social conditions for the development of science and Ips globally, and their development and form in some specific countries. Next, some more specific issues relating to Ips are discussed. These issues include the nature of Ips, scientific standards, type of culture concept favored, views on the philosophy of science, understanding of mainstream psychology, generalization of findings, and Ips' isolation and independence. Finally, conclusions are drawn, for example with respect to the future of IP.

Keywords: indigenous psychology, culture, anthropology of knowledge, review, psychology

Isbns: 9781108461689 (PB), 9781108562171 (OC)
Issns: 2515-3986 (online), 2515-3943 (print)

Contents

Indigenous psychologies (Ips) represent an approach to research in psychology which stresses the importance of research being grounded in the conditions of the researcher's own society and culture, for example with respect to research problems, research methods, research instruments, assumptions, concepts, and theories. They exist predominantly in non-Western countries. Numerous researchers have argued that this approach is needed due to the dominance of Western culture in mainstream psychology (the dominant form of psychology) and the poor fit of this psychology to the realities in the IP researchers' countries (e.g., Enriquez, 1977; Ho, 1998; D. Sinha, 1993, 1997; Yang, 2012). Western psychology is often marked by individualism, liberal values, and an alienated attitude to religion (e.g., Kim, 1995; D. Sinha & M. Sinha, 1997). Moreover, Yang (2012, p. 4) described psychological research in non-Western countries prior to indigenization as "a sheer mimic of Western psychology" and as "misplaced, dislocated, and decontextualized" (p. 15).

In line with this, a further argument for the need for Ips is the perceived lack of usefulness of results from Western mainstream psychology: that is, they do not replicate well in non-Western countries. Results based on the premises of the culture in the IP researchers' own societies are more useful for solving problems in those societies. For example, Yang (2012, p. 11) argued that IP is needed in non-Western countries because of its greater success in "understanding, explaining, and predicting local people's mind and behavior as well as solving their personal and social problems." Moreover, there is a lack of research on phenomena that are of importance for non-Western, often developing, countries, such as research on one-child families, effects on children of sibling caretaking, poverty, and analphabetism. Finally, Ips are also needed because they contribute to a more complete understanding of the human being and thereby to the development of a truly global psychology (e.g., Berry & Kim, 1993). The development of Ips has taken place in a larger national and global context, and this Element provides a discussion of the nature and challenges of IP from the perspectives of *science studies* and *anthropology of knowledge* (the study of human understanding in its social context).

After a general introduction, I first describe the general social conditions for the development of science and IP globally, and then the conditions in some countries where they have developed. Next, I deal with events associated with Ips at the international level. I discuss a number of unresolved issues and challenges for Ips, such as their nature, the type of culture concept appropriate for these psychologies, scientific standards, issues in the philosophy of science, generalization of findings, and issues of isolation and independence. Finally, I draw some conclusions with respect to the nature, development, and future of the Ips.

Social science develops as a response to factors relating to internal developments in a discipline, and as an effect of changes in the social reality external to
the discipline (Yearley, 2005). The IPs – an academic and intellectual movement reacting to Western mainstream psychology, mostly in non-Western
countries – clearly illustrate the latter type of factors in that their origin is
associated with global historical events. However, development of specific IPs
has also been influenced by local conditions in national contexts. An unknown
amount of research literature pertaining to IPs is published in the IP researchers' mother tongue or national language, which are usually languages other
than English. In addition, there exists an international literature written in
English relating to IPs, including descriptions of their research programs,
character, history, empirical results, and methodology, and the Element is
based on this literature.

The term *indigenous psychology* has been used in different ways. First, it can
denote the type of psychology that is the object of this Element – that is, mostly
non-Western psychologies that *have explicitly declared themselves as indigenous psychologies*, in contrast to the Western/US "mainstream" psychology –
that is, scientific, but grounded in a specific society's culture. Second, the term
indigenous psychology is used to mean traditional ideas about psychology
developed in most societies, religions, and philosophies – for example, theories
and concepts about the nature of the human being. Third, the term is used as a
label for all modern psychologies, including Western mainstream psychology.
This use points out that all psychologies come from a local cultural context and
in this sense are indigenous. Thus, many authors (e.g., Kim & Berry, 1993a;
Poortinga, 1999) have argued that modern mainstream Western psychology is
foremost a product of Western culture and is therefore an indigenous psychology. An interesting illustration of this third use is specific, locally based
psychologies that have developed semi-independently of mainstream Western
psychology, such as the Soviet cultural-historical school in the 1930s and
liberation psychology in Latin America.

Science studies and *the anthropology of knowledge* are overlapping perspectives that are used in this Element. Science studies is a cross-disciplinary
enterprise that provides descriptive studies of research activities, meaning
that the object of study is research as actually carried out by researchers.
Various schools in the sociology of knowledge have been influential in this
work (Sismondo, 2004; Yearley, 2005). Adair (2006) and Gabrenya, Kung, and
Chen (2006) have studied specific IPs from the perspective of the social studies
of science. Moreover, other IP authors have recommended such studies (e.g.,
Yang, 2012). The anthropology of knowledge has a broader mission in that it is
the general study of the development of human understanding in its social

context. This includes studies of how understanding from one society is inter-preted, understood, and modified in other societies (Allwood, 2013a; Barth, 2002). IPs illustrate how such reception is dependent on the local conditions at the receiving end.

The Western dominance in psychology is illustrated by a study reported by Garcia-Martinez, Guerro-Bote, and de Moya-Anegón (2012). Using Scopus (Elsevier) as a data source, the world's largest scientific database (in English), and studying the period 2003–2008, these authors found that just 69% of the world's countries publish in psychology. The production of scientific works is even more skewed; the forty most productive countries published 98.3% of all research documents in psychology. As expected, the USA ranked highest, produ-cing 43% of all the world's research documents, followed by the UK and Canada. These three countries together published more than 60% of all research docu-ments; including Germany, Austria, and the Netherlands brings the figure to more than 70%. China ranked 24th and India 32nd. A group made up of fourteen countries accounted for 82.1% of the total production in psychology. Apart from the six countries mentioned above, this group also included Switzerland, Sweden, New Zealand, Israel, Finland, Belgium, Norway, and Hong Kong – all Western (or Westernized) countries, more or less. The results for citations (49.2% US), journals (66.6% US, 20% UK, and 14.5% the Netherlands), and institutions were in line with those for publications.

The Western and US dominance in psychology is also well documented by Arnett (2008), who showed that from 2003–2007, 96% of the participants in the studies reported in six top US psychology journals came from Western coun-tries where 12% of the world's population lives. Similarly, Henrich, Heine, and Norenzayan (2010) observed that a great majority of the studies in psychology have students as participants, representing a very low proportion of the earth's population with respect to their social position and economy. However, it is also of interest that Adair et al. (2009), in a comparative study, found indica-tions that, related to the rest of the world, the proportion of psychology research produced in the USA is slowly decreasing. One effect of Western dominance is that other cultural perspectives have had little chance to influence the develop-ment of psychology.

1 General Background Conditions for the Development of IPs

The development of an IP in a country demands sufficiently evolved general conditions for research. However, such general conditions are often insuffi-ciently developed for psychology in many parts of the world.

Basalla (1967) provided a useful general scheme (model) for the historical spread of Western science. This scheme has three, often overlapping stages. It applies foremost to the situation in non-Western countries, but stages 2 and 3 also cover, for example, US physics in relation to Europe in the nineteenth century.

As noted, Basalla's model is explicitly focused on Western science, but in general it is questionable to assert that science *started* in the West. Claiming that science started in the West would be tantamount to neglecting the cultural interactions and influences that have historically existed between the various parts of the globe – for example, between Europe and different parts of Asia – and thus to neglect all the different contributions to humankind's knowledge and understanding by different societies (see, e.g., Goonatilake, 1998). However, workers in the West can be said to have added crucial components to science.

In Basalla's first stage (not named), non-Western countries simply provide resources for European, or Western, science[1]. In the beginning, data often related to flora, fauna, and geography is collected by Western explorers and their non-Western assistants. In the second stage, *colonial science*, non-Western researchers in a discipline are dependent on the research community in one or more European, or at least Western, countries. This stage applies whether the country was a formal Western colony or not. Moghaddam and Taylor (1985) noted that non-Western universities were mostly simply copied from the Western world – for example, with respect to how they were organized, their curricula, their equipment, and their values. During this stage the (mostly non-Western) researchers in the dependent country tend to get their PhD education in the West, attempt to publish in Western-based scientific journals, are members of Western scientific societies, and follow the development of research produced in the Western-based research community. Using an example from the late nineteenth and early twentieth centuries, Basalla (1967, p. 614) noted that "[h]undreds of American chemists, physicists and biologists ... pursued graduate studies, or gained PhD's, at Berlin, Leipzig, Göttingen, Heidelberg, Munich, or Paris." At the same time many students from other countries (e.g., more than 600 from Japan) were sent to be trained in Europe and the USA. In brief, in Basalla's second stage, the research community and home-base of researchers from dependent countries is to a large extent in the West.

In the third and final stage, *independent scientific tradition*, the (typically) non-Western nation establishes a full-fledged research community of its own,

---

[1] In this text I will not distinguish "science" (as in natural science) from other types of research.

including its own institutions and PhD educations. This stage is associated with attempts at nation building. Establishing a national research community will, according to Basalla, include overcoming resistance to science, for example in the influential elite parts of society. It also includes a need to create sufficiently high status for researchers, so that the state is willing to provide their wages and to establish an educational system that provides enough relevantly educated students for postgraduate study programs that are sufficiently developed to be provided in the homeland. It also includes a need to build up national scientific organizations and open ways to allow researchers to communicate nationally and internationally. This includes setting up and maintaining the organization of scientific journals and conference programs, both in the national language(s) and in English.

Although not much elaborated by Basalla, this work would also include the delicate task of building a relevant peer-review culture for the discipline in question. Saberwal (1982) described the difficulties in Indian anthropology and sociology of developing a critical and independent peer-review culture based on shared scientific values. A decade later, J. B. P. Sinha (1995) made similar observations on the situation for psychology in India. In this context he quoted conclusions by Dalal (1990): "reviews of articles in India are likely to reflect the status of the person whose work is being reviewed and/or the relationship between the author and reviewer" (p. 748).

Moreover, disciplines have different material needs with respect to their technological base (Basalla, 1967). For example, physics (especially in modern times) often needs expensive – sometimes very expensive – equipment (e.g., particle accelerators). In contrast, the material needs of psychology are more modest: functioning computers for data analyses and for text production (albeit this demands functioning electricity), access to electronic libraries, printers, and paper for printers. However, psychology is often prioritized only after the needs of the natural sciences have been met (see, e.g., Adair, 1995). In general, non-Western IPs lack economic resources and are therefore dependent on the West for their functionality (Shams, 2002). To illustrate, as Mayer (2002) described the situation in Nigeria around the year 2000, "[t]here are frequent electric power cuts, poor postal and telephone services and acute shortage of water" (p. 4). In addition, in many non-Western countries the number of hours that researchers at universities must spend teaching is very high, and the level of research grants available in psychology is very low. Such a situation obviously makes the conditions for developing an IP very difficult!

2 Specific Conditions for the Development of IPs

Three initial observations can be made with respect to the development of IPs. First, as noted by non-Western IP authors (e.g., Nsamenang, 2013; D. Sinha, 1986), traditional IPs, consisting of theories and concepts developed in their communities (i.e., IPs in the second version of the concept *indigenous psychologies* discussed above), were developed before the arrival of Western psychology. Second, development of IPs, although dependent on the last two stages of Basalla's model, includes further tasks for the researchers, namely to develop a new conceptual and methodological base ·for their research and to develop new organizational structures – that is, to create a discipline based on, and integrated in, the society's own culture and social structure. The third observation is that the indigenization process frequently must be carried out in a situation where the third stage in Basalla's model has not been fully accomplished.

John Adair, a Canadian researcher, has described the general conditions for the development of IPs and has reviewed the development of IPs in various texts (1992, 1996, 1998, 1999, 2006). In Adair's approach, IPs are seen as cultural-social phenomena that develop in an open, historically situated context. Four steps in the indigenization process are recognized by Adair: 1) importation, 2) implantation, 3) indigenization, and 4) autochthonization. Adair's third and fourth steps often occur in parallel. Adair later added a step he calls *internationalization*, which includes international presence and visibility, collaborations, and contributions (Adair et al., 2006).

The main difference between Adair's model and stages 2 and 3 in Basalla's model is that Adair has inserted the step *indigenization* between Basalla's stages 2 and 3. By complete *autochthonization* of the discipline, Adair means that it functions completely self-sufficiently in the country. That is, it has its own PhD education, journals, research funding, and critical mass of researchers. Adair's step 4 is like Basalla's stage 3, except that it specifically concerns the indigenization process of psychology.

Adair (1996) described the distinction between *indigenization* and *endogenization*, where indigenization means modifying a psychology developed elsewhere with respect to its discipline and methods so that they fit the new culture. Endogenization means "developing an entirely new or different discipline from within the culture" (p. 51). As will become clear, in many (maybe most) countries the indigenization process in Adair's sense is not completed. Moreover, Yang (2012, p. 10) argues that the indigenization process cannot be as complete as Western psychology, which is developed by endogenization.

Indigenized knowledge "tends to be moderately contextualized" (Yang, 2012, p. 15). Yang's reasons for this are that indigenization is carried out in relation to an already-present Westernized psychology, and the mainstream Western psychology is concurrently present during the indigenization process and continues to influence the psychology being developed. A final reason is that the researchers working with indigenizing psychology in their country will, when doing this, be opposed by some of the other psychologists in their country who continue to carry out Westernized research. Thus, due to the fact that Westernized psychology in different ways hinders the development of IP (what Yang calls "indigenized psychology," or IZP), "[the] IZP will never become as genuine and pure an IP as the one that spontaneously developed in Euro-American societies" (Yang, 2012, p. 11).

In general, the development of IPs is a process that has occurred on both the national level and the international levels. In Sections 2 and 3, we first examine examples of development of IPs in specific countries, and then review developments at the international level. However, in addition to this, the *interactions* that have taken place between the national and the international levels are important. Historically, psychological researchers have interacted at an international level where they have communicated and organized themselves. However, such international interactions have often not been equal, because Western researchers for a long time, and maybe even today, have had access to more economic resources and to a better-developed and more organized discipline. Still, much of the substantial international collaboration with respect to the development of IPs may have been more democratic.

In brief, some common denominators in the developments of the respective IPs can be discerned. Early on, European psychology was exported to the USA, and soon US psychology began to be exported to Europe, while at the same time Western psychology was exported to the rest of the world through colonial and imperialistic processes, including exportation of the Western educational system. Yang (2012) gave a more peaceful description of this process, in that he did not mention the influence of colonialism and imperialism when he described the introduction of Western psychology into non-Western countries. Although the conditions for development of IPs differ between countries, a common denominator of many (although not necessarily all) IPs is that they "can be viewed as a re-affirmation of a nation-inspired identity achieved in the process of a national democratic struggle" (San Juan, 2006, p. 53; for an opposite view, see Yang, 2012).

Next, I provide some country-specific examples of the development of IPs. These examples are not necessarily completely representative for all IPs.

Instead, the IPs described are chosen to provide some of the general picture and to illustrate some of the important variations in IPs.

Generally speaking, by studying variations in IPs it is possible to learn about their nature – or at least we can consider whether there is an inherent nature to IP or if different IPs are simply functions of their current circumstances. In brief, different types of IPs have developed as an effect of their path-dependencies. Although I have attempted to describe important conditions, the descriptions of specific countries in Sections 2.1–2.10 may unfortunately have missed some important events in the development of IPs. Furthermore, in addition, it will be evident that some individually very engaged researchers have, at least to some extent, put their hallmark on specific IPs. The following types of IPs are described: South and East Asian IPs (with subtypes), Nationalistic IPs (e.g., the Philippines), IPs in the Muslim world (specifically in Iran), Oceanian (e.g., Australian and New Zealand) and "4th world" IPs, very small-size IPs (e.g., African IPs in the Cameroon and Ghana), and Western IPs (e.g., Canadian). These types of IP are at different levels, and occasionally an IP fits into more than one of these categories.

The South and East Asian IPs, including those in India, the Philippines, and Taiwan, tend to be among the best-established and most active IPs. Among these, IP in the Philippines was among the first to develop (Ho, 1998), and this is described first and in most detail. After this, the remaining IPs to be described will be described in a more or less east–west order.

2.1 Philippines

The Philippines has a long colonial history; it was colonialized by Spain in the sixteenth century and was ruled by the USA from 1898 to 1946. Finally, the Republic of the Philippines was declared in 1946. With this background, and maybe influenced by the massive liberation of African states from colonialism in the 1960s, in the 1970s there was a wave of nationalism in the Philippines which influenced the demand for indigenization of psychology. Many authors (e.g., Church & Katigbak, 2002; Gastardo-Conaco, 2005; Pe-Pua, 2015; Pe-Pua & Protacio-Marcelino, 2000; San Juan, 2006) have described the development of IP in the Philippines. D. Sinha (1997) argued that the indigenization of psychology in the Philippines was the strongest in Asia.

There were early negative observations about the fit of Western psychology and other social research with conditions in the Philippines. For example,

Protacio-De Castro (in Allwood & Berry, 2006) noted that Feliciano in 1965 observed that the research methods used in Western social science did not fit well in the rural Philippines. In the 1970s the psychologist Virgilio Enriquez, with colleagues, advocated the need for an IP in the Philippines. Enriquez, commonly recognized as the pioneer of IP development in the Philippines, took his PhD at Northwestern University in the USA in 1971 and then returned to the Philippines. Enriquez's role as founding father of IP in the Philippines is reflected in the title of a paper by Pe-Pua and Protacio-Marcelino in 2000: "Sikolohiyang Pilipino (Filipino psychology): A legacy to Virgilio Enriquez." Similarly, Pe-Pua (2015, p. 789) called Enriquez "the forefather of IP in the Philippines." At the time Enriquez returned to the Philippines there was a wave of intense nationalism in the country. This nationalism included questioning of everything foreign (Gastardo-Conaco, 2005). Enriquez (1977) argued that social scientists in the Philippines had a responsibility to contribute to "the understanding of the psychology of the Filipino in particular and Filipino society and culture in general" (p. 3). The new psychology was named *Sikolohiyang Pilipino* (SP, Filipino psychology) and was defined by Enriquez as a "psychology based on the experience, ideas and orientation of the Filipino" (1994, cited in Church & Katigbak, 2002, p. 131). Ho (1998, p. 95) characterized Enriquez's vision of indignization as a "political agenda" and, similarly, Church and Katigbak (2002, p. 131) concluded that many SP texts have "a strong and explicit sociopolitical thrust."

Importantly, SP psychology would "protest against a psychology that perpetuates the colonial status of the Filipino mind, the exploitation of the masses, and the imposition of psychologies developed in industrialized countries" (Church & Katigbak, 2002, p. 131). Further, Enriquez (Church & Katigbak, 2002) described the new psychology as emphasizing national identity, social engagement, language and culture, and different types of applications in, for example, health and agricultural practices. Other recommended fields of application were art, religion, and mass media (Church & Katigbak, 2002; Pe-Pua & Protacio-Marcelino, 2000). As part of the assumptions of SP, Enriquez (1977, p. 3) noted that "[The Filipino's] consciousness of being a Filipino psychologically defines him as one, no matter how he sees and defines the Filipino." He added that the nation level provides a possibility for people to develop a broader consciousness "as he hurdles his sub-national regional identity towards a national identity" (p. 4). In this context, Enriquez (1977, p. 6) used the concept *Filipino mass consciousness.*

Thus, an important part of SP is to describe the individual Filipino's awareness of, and identification with, the Filipino national identity. Furthermore, an important aim of SP is to correct previous conceptions of the "national traits" of the Filipino human being. San Juan (2006) observed that this implies that "the natives have suddenly bolted from slumber, it seems, and have begun to interpolate their own translation, and, in effect, represent themselves" (p. 50).

Moreover, SP was to focus on developing a psychology that is applicable in the concrete Filipino practice, and the methods in SP should fit the social context. The relation between the researcher and the participant(s) is emphasized, and should be based on equality and protect the participants' welfare (e.g., Pe-Pua & Protacio-Marcelino, 2000). In an early development in the 1970s, Santiago argued that explicit and clear research designs are not needed and that it is not necessary to review the research literature before starting research (Pe-Pua & Protacio-Marcelino, 2000). Pe-Pua & Protacio-Marcelino also noted that what is called the *pakapa-kapa perspective* has been adopted in SP research, and they quote Torres' description from 1982 of this perspective as "an approach characterized by groping, searching and probing into an unsystematized mass of social and cultural data to obtain order, meaning and directions for research" (p. 59). Enriquez (1993) also argued for the use of "objective" research methods and that the approach should be what he described as "total." As an illustration of a research method developed in SP, Enriquez (1993) described *Pagtatanung-tanong* (asking around), as "essentially a cross between surveys and informant interviewing" (p. 166). In this method, the same question is answered by different persons, and the participants know that other people have answered the same question. SP has involved investigation of a number of Filipino concepts, using a cross-disciplinary approach involving anthropology, linguistics, and philosophy, and it has debated how central specific concepts are to the Filipino mind.

With respect to the national character of the Filipino, as recounted by Protacio-De Castro (in Allwood & Berry, 2006, p. 252), Enriquez wanted SP to focus "on that which truly defines a Filipino: his sense of *pakikipagkapwa* (his 'me/other' orientation or shared identity)." Similarly, according to Church and Katigbak (2002, p. 133), Enriquez argued that "kapwa," which he interpreted as "the recognition of shared identity with others," was "the core concept underlying Filipino interpersonal behavior." In general, SP is filled with debates and controversies (see Pe-Pua, 2015). For example, Enriquez's interpretation of the concept "kapwa" has been contested by other Filipino researchers who have suggested alternative interpretations.

Early on, Enriquez introduced the distinction between *indigenization from without*, called *exogenous* indigenization, and *indigenization from within*, called *endogenous* indigenization (Pe-Pua, 2015). Exogenous indigenization starts from outside of the researched culture, and the aim is to create a version of the foreign materials that fits the IP researcher's country (Pe-Pua, 2015). Such materials could be tests, theories, and studies, usually from the West. Endogenous indigenization, also called "cultural revalidation" by Pe-Pua and Protacio-Marcelino (2000), uses the indigenous culture as a source of concepts and methods. As described by Pe-Pua (2015, p. 789), "[t]his path involves processes such as semantic elaboration, indigenous codification or recodification, and systematic explication of implied theoretical frameworks, to produce knowledge that reflects the indigenous experience and realities." Enriquez also argued that the Filipino language was the perfect tool for understanding what he called the Filipino diwa (essence). In addition, he argued that this language should be used for teaching psychology. By developing SP, Filipino researchers would also help to create a psychology that is truly universal (Protacio-De Castro, in Allwood & Berry, 2006).

There have been different types of critique levelled against SP (e.g., Church & Katigbak, 2002; Gastardo-Conaco, 2005; San Juan, 2006). Church and Katigbak (2002) summarized critiques by themselves and other researchers of SP research methods. For example, they noted that Filipino researchers have worried about subjectivity and data contamination in SP. Furthermore, they argued that many of the methods developed are similar to conventional ethnographic methods such as naturalistic observation and are not really new. They also observed that qualitative phenomenological methods have become more popular. Similarly, some of the methods from SF described by Ho (1998) are highly reminiscent of a simpler version of grounded theory and of phenomenological research methods developed in Western psychology. Church and Katigbak (2002, p. 129) also argued that the "insularity and the limited research culture" of SP are risks to further progress. For example, some researchers in the *Sikolohiyang Pilipino* movement have argued that the results of Filipino psychology should only be published in the Philippine language. This would seriously decrease contributions to the international research literature.

An important aspect of SP, as noted above, is its nationalistic and political aspects. San Juan (2006) described SP as a response "to continuing US interference in Philippine society, culture and politics" (p. 53). Church and Katigbak (2002) argued that this is problematic in that the influence of sociopolitical factors when selecting methods and when analyzing indigenous concepts could seriously threat SP's scientific objectivity. More generally, the authors questioned whether SP's clearly evidenced sociopolitical ambitions were compatible with developing a scientific IP.

Similarly the goal of SP to describe the Filipino personality has been questioned. For example, Protacio-De Castro noted that, given the many Philippine ethnic groups, it is not clear who exactly should count as "the Filipino," and remarked: "In a country of multiple ethnicities, this is a valid point" (in Allwood & Berry, 2006, p. 253). This issue is highly relevant since there are currently more than 180 ethnic groups in the Philippines (Wikipedia, https://en.wikipedia.org/wiki/Ethnic_groups_in_the_Philippines, retrieved 19 February, 2018). More than 50% of these ethnic groups have a language that belongs to a unique linguistic group. Gastardo-Conaco (2005) deplored that groups other than those of Tagalog ethnicity were so poorly represented in SP, and also argued that gender differences should be better represented in SP. Along the same lines, San Juan (2006, p. 63) wrote: "This drive to posit a unitary society based on a supposedly uniform physiognomy or national character that transcends class boundaries . . . betokens a kind of unwarranted populist idealism that discourages critical inquiry." The issue of how to describe and represent a smaller or larger number of cultures within a country with respect to their characteristics in a common summary frame is, if it is worth doing, relevant to other IPs too.

It is difficult to appraise the current status of SP. Despite the vigorous activity associated with the development of SP with respect to related publishing and organizing societies, there are, according to Gastardo-Conaco (2005), signs of stagnation. Examples are a slower rate of publication and the fact that the field has become somewhat less visible. Moreover, Church and Katigbak (2002) reported that SP is treated as a separate subject in university departments in the Philippines. This is noticeable, for example, in that psychology departments' classifications of student essays list SP work in a separate category from essays relating to other types of psychology. Pe-Pua (2015), writing more broadly, also observed that indigenization from without has been the most common way to develop IP in India, Taiwan, and the Philippines.

2.2 Taiwan

IP in Taiwan shows a somewhat similar developmental history to IP in the Philippines, but also has its own characteristic features. Due to national and international political events in the 1940s and '50s, psychology in Taiwan was very tightly linked to US psychology: American textbooks were used, and students usually went to the USA for education (Hwang, 2005;

Yang, 1997). The department of psychology at the National Taiwan University (NTU) was established in 1949 as the first psychology department in Taiwan, discounting an earlier psychological laboratory that was established by two Japanese researchers in order to study the aborigines (Hwang, 2005). According to its homepage (www.psy.ntu.edu.tw/index.php/department/aboutus, retrieved 19 February, 2018), the NTU department is the leading psychology department in Taiwan. Its master's program started in 1961, and the PhD program in 1971. The situation changed somewhat when the PRC (People's Republic of China) took over Taiwan's seat in the UN, but Hwang (2005) still described the Taiwanese psychology of the 1970s as a "transplant" of Western psychology, and he cited studies showing that even in the 1990s Taiwanese psychological studies showed heavy dependence on US psychological research. The research mostly used students and post hoc interpretations of the data. Hwang concluded that "[r]esearch of this type not only lacks theoretical meaning, but also has few connections to people in the local society" (p. 230).

Kuo-Shu Yang was a pioneer of IP in Taiwan. He took his PhD in 1969 at the University of Illinois, USA, with Harry Triandis as supervisor, and then returned to Taiwan (Gabrenya & Sun, 2015). According to his own account (1997), Yang conducted psychological research in the traditional Western way until about 1976, but in that year he changed his research approach due to psychology's dislocation with Chinese reality and its lack of connection with his Chinese background. In 1976 he embarked upon a mission to *Sinicize* psychology. However, he soon realized that he would not get support from his colleagues at the NTU, and instead approached colleagues in other social sciences such as anthropology and sociology. After having worked one year in Hong Kong, in 1981 he participated in organizing a conference on the Sinicization of social and behavioral science. At this stage he still thought that there was "only one scientific psychology and that it was not legitimate to talk about indigenous psychology within that psychology" (Yang, 1997, pp. 67–68). He further explained that his ambition for IP at that time was for it to be a simple descriptive psychology that would use folk concepts of the kind explored in cultural anthropology. At this time he used the term "Sinicization of psychology" and started a research group on this theme. By Sinicization of psychology Yang meant studies of features common to all Chinese societies. However, in 1986 he radicalized his approach, and at the same time started to use the term "indigenous psychology." By indigenous psychology Yang now meant studies of common features of all Chinese societies, but also studies of "the unique psychological and behavioural aspects of people in a certain Chinese society" (1997, p. 69). After this, the work to indigenize psychology in Taiwan gathered speed. A research laboratory for IP was established, as was the journal *Indigenous Psychological Research*, in 1993.

IP in Taiwan has also been characterized by debates on what type(s) of IP should be developed. Here, the distinction made by Virgio Enriquez between *exogenous* indigenization and *endogenous* indigenization is useful. As noted earlier, *exogenous* indigenization means a type of indigenization process where foreign thinking (typically Western) is used as a basis for the development of the country's IP; by *endogenous* indigenization is meant indigenization *from within* – that is, where no foreign thinking is used in the indigenization process. Yang (see Hwang, 2005) wrote in 1993 that endogenous psychology was the type of IP he wanted to develop. In contrast, Hwang (e.g., 2005, 2015) has repeatedly argued that IP in Taiwan and elsewhere should be based on a methodo-logical and philosophical platform from the West – that is, an *exogenous* type of indigenization process.

Both Yang and Hwang have been very productive researchers. Yang and co-workers have published, among other things, research on Chinese reactions to modernization, Chinese personality, and various Chinese folk concepts. Hwang and co-workers have published extensively on Chinese modernization and on concepts deriving from Confucianism and how these should be understood (see, e.g., Hwang, 2006).

The current state of IP in Taiwan is somewhat unclear. Gabrenya et al. (2006) studied attitudes toward IP (called the Taiwan Indigenous Psychology Movement, TIPM) among psychology researchers (the data collection took place from 1998–2000) in Taiwan. Their results showed that the TIPM was well known and had moderate support. However, there were also a number of researchers opposed to the TIPM. Gabrenya et al. (2006) noted that IP is mostly present at institutions in northern Taiwan. Looking at the homepage of the psychology department at NTU in November 2017, it is difficult to find any information about activities connected with Taiwanese IP. For example, the word "indigenous" and associated terms are missing.

Moreover, Yang (2012, p. 23) urged that TIPM should give "priority to the study of local people's culturally unique psychological and behavioral phe-nomena." However, the extent to which this includes, for example, Taiwan's indigenous groups (16 recognized and other not formally recognized indigen-ous groups, equating to approximately 2% of the population) is unclear. In general, the future of IP in Taiwan is difficult to predict, and the extent to which there is a new generation of IP researchers ready to carry on the pioneering work started by Yang and Hwang is not clear.

2.3 China

The situation for IP in China (PRC) differs from that in Taiwan. Whereas IP in Taiwan developed early, there has been very little explicit activity associated with the label "indigenous psychology" in China, as evidenced, for example, in Jing and Fu's (2001) review paper on modern Chinese psychology. Jing and Fu described the development of psychology in China as starting with ancient Chinese philosophy (including Confucius), and as influenced by Jesuit missionaries in the sixteenth century. According to the same authors, modern psychological development started with Chinese researchers spending time in the West after the establishment of Wundt's psychological laboratory in Leipzig in 1879, and then bringing psychology back to China. *The Chinese Psychological Society* was founded in 1921. After the Communist takeover in China in 1949, it was decided that Chinese psychology should be guided by Marxist dialectical materialism, and conditioned reflexes were taken "as the physiological basis of human behavior" (Jing & Fu, 2001, p. 414). Western psychology was criticized on ideological grounds as too individualistic and paying too little heed to social influences on behavior. During the Cultural Revolution, psychology was not practiced. Later, Leung and Zhang (1995), with respect to the situation for psychology in China, wrote "[e]ven though it is a science, psychology could be construed as an ideology and hence a threat to the doctrine promulgated by a ruling regime or by influential segments of a society" (p. 694).

After the Cultural Revolution psychology was rehabilitated and Western psychology was introduced. Jing and Fu (2001) noted that, by 2001, Chinese psychology had contributed to various fields within the discipline, and the conditions for research were described as favorable due to the government's provision of financial resources. At that time, psychology in China was described as poorly adapted to the needs of Chinese society since it had been developed in advanced industrial countries. Jing and Fu also argued that Chinese psychology too often simply replicated previous Western research, and that it did not relate sufficiently to Chinese needs. Instead, they suggested, psychologists in China should learn how to study issues related to the quick pace of change in China. They also recommended case studies of important local events and phenomena.

These observations might have been written by an IP author in, for example, Taiwan or India, but the idea of IP was not reviewed or discussed by Jing and Fu. Why might this be? When I visited China in 2005, I asked researchers about the apparent absence of IP in China and asked them why. The explanation I got was "that's what they do in Taiwan!" However, it is interesting to note that

Professor Henry Kao, from the department of psychology at Sun Yat-Sen University, Guanzhou, China (in Allwood & Berry, 2006), very clearly pointed to activities initiated from Hong Kong and especially Taiwan as important for the development of Chinese IP. Such influence may to some extent have been due to the efforts of Yang and the cross-cultural psychologist Michael Bond, who has held a long employment in Hong Kong.

2.4 South Korea

IP in South Korea seems to have had a slow start. For example, Choi, Kim, and Choi (1993) had little to report about IP in South Korea. However, Uichol Kim, who did his PhD with John Berry in Canada, has since played an important role in the development of Korean IP. For example, Kim, Park, and Park (1999) presented what they called a Korean IP as an *alternative paradigm* (in contrast to what they called "traditional psychology" – i.e., Western psychology). In addition, the authors noted that "Korean indigenous psychology advocates a *transaction model* of causality that focuses on the generative and proactive aspects. Bandura's (1997) sociocognitive theory shares many of the basic scientific tenets of Korean indigenous psychology" (pp. 457–458).

Moreover, Korean IP, according to the same authors, encompasses three levels of analysis: the physiological, the psychological, and the collective level. The collective level is not a mere sum of its individual properties, it is an "emergent property." The authors stated that Korean IP will examine everyday concepts and collective representations as a first step, and Kim, Park, and Park (2000) observed that Korean IP is an example of an *indigenization from within* approach. Moreover, Kim and Park (in Allwood & Berry, 2006, p. 250) asserted that in South Korea IP is the same as cultural psychology. Kim and Park (2006, p. 33) presented a very similar approach, "the transactional approach," as a general approach to IP. In this approach "individuals are viewed as agents of their action and collective agents through their culture (Kim, 1999, 2000, 2001)." However, the current status of IP in South Korea has been difficult to ascertain.

2.5 India

Although also associated with nationalistic sentiments, IP in India has a different character than Filipino SP. Durganand Sinha, the pioneer of IP in India, suggested (1997, p. 134) that "indigenization is an ongoing process rather than a finished product; it is gradual and comes about in stages." Sinha (1986) described the indigenization process in India as occurring in four phases. Phase 1 corresponds to the pre-independence era and phase 2 to the postindependence period up to the 1960s. The third phase, called *the phase of problem-oriented research*, lasted up to approximately 1980, when it was followed by phase 4, *the indigenization phase*.

In phase 1, the first Indian university department of psychology was established in 1916, but often psychology was part of philosophy departments and separate departments of psychology only became more common between the 1940s and 1960s (Misra & Paranjpe, 2012). The *Indian Journal of Psychology* was founded in 1926 (J. B. P. Sinha, 1995). However, students interested in modern psychology often went to the West (Britain or the United States) to study for their PhD. After their return to India, these researchers adhered to the learned Western type of research in a servile manner (D. Sinha, 1993). Sinha noted that this showed the West's political domination over the Third World and that it was a part of modernization and Westernization. In Sinha's phase 2, starting after the Indian independence from Britain in 1947, efforts to indigenize psychology in India began to emerge (Sinha, 1993). The philosopher and historian of science, Dhruv Raina, noted (1997) that, following independence, India attempted to reconstruct its identity on its own terms and not in terms of the orientalist and colonial image provided by the West. Moreover, "[w]hat was found problematic was the insertion within an internationalist context of a canonized European definition of rationality and universality" (p. 18). The indigenization movement was to a large extent a reaction to this situation. On a similar note, Sinha (1993, p. 33) noted that after 1947 there was a "growth of national pride and a gradual awareness of distinct identity among scholars who began to feel the need for 'outgrowing the alien framework.'" Thus, efforts to indigenize psychology in India were initiated as part of generalized social processes prevailing in the country, which also affected other social sciences such as sociology and social anthropology (Raina, 1997; Saberwal, 1982).

Sinha's phase 3 was marked by researchers becoming more aware of the need for applied research that generated results that were usable in the local context. As a result of this, the period was also marked by a "realization of the limitations of their studies which had been excessively dependent on the West" (1986, p. 43). The importance of research investigating the specific local conditions pertaining where the research results were to be applied is illustrated by results reported by Wagner et al. (1999). This study showed that people utilized both modern Westernized and traditional conceptualizations of madness, depending on the context activated by the person.

Durganand Sinha had a large impact on Indian IP. He was born in Northeastern Bihar and took his MSc in psychology at Cambridge, UK, in

1949, where the social memory psychologist Frederic Bartlett was his mentor. Early on, Sinha studied memory and cognition by use of experimental methods. However, he had broad interests, as illustrated by his early study "Behavior in a catastrophic situation: A psychological study of reports and rumors," published in the *British Journal of Psychology* in 1952. After returning to India in 1949 (Pandey, 1998), Sinha started research in various overlapping areas, such as village studies, social change, psychology of poverty and deprivation, rural leadership, student unrest, changes in the Indian family, value change over generations, and childhood fears. These studies likely made him acutely aware that, in order to be relevant, the psychological approach should be adapted to local conditions, and in his research he often adopted and expanded Western models. For example, in his research on poverty and deprivation, he elaborated Bronfenbrenner's model to fit better in the Indian context (Misra, 1998).

Sinha worked at Allahabad University from 1961 and founded the psychology department there. From the middle of the 1960s, he began to strongly advocate for a culturally and socially appropriate psychology, and from the mid-1980s for Indian indigenous psychology (Pandey, 1998). Sinha has argued for a broadened conception of psychology, focusing on the phenomenon studied rather than the constraints imposed by the psychological discipline (e.g., D. Sinha, 1993). He also (e.g., 1997) argued for *indigenization from within* by means of an *indigenized approach to knowledge*. Such an approach "places particular emphasis on culture-specific factors in human functioning – the researcher wants to know what is native, or rooted in specific societies and cultures" (p. 131). Sinha founded the journal *Psychology and Developing Societies* in 1981 and was later involved in helping to found various organizations at the national and international levels. For example, he was a founding member of the *International Association of Cross-Cultural Psychology* (IACCP).

The fourth phase – *the indigenization phase* – was characterized by Sinha (1986, p. 63) as a phase "of questioning, doubt and a search for a new identity." J. B. P. Sinha (in Allwood & Berry, 2006; see also D. Sinha, 1997) reported that in the 1980s the indigenization of Indian psychology gathered speed. In this phase, Indian IP started to integrate ideas, concepts, and methods from India with those from abroad. Skepticism toward Western psychology intensified; for example, Western psychology was increasingly believed to be inappropriate as a guide for data collection, especially when studying Indian participants (D. Sinha, 1986). Poortinga (2016, p. 162) summarized Sinha's fourth stage as a "confident acceptance of the indigenous and open to blending with Western elements."

The poor fit between Western mainstream psychology and realities in India was noticed early by funding agencies. In 1973, the *Review Committee of the Indian Council of Social Science Research* wrote of "concern about the foreignness of social science research in India in the field of psychology in particular" (quoted in Sinha, 1993, p. 31). This concern was reiterated three decades later in *The Pondicherry Manifesto of Indian Psychology*, issued in 2002 in the context of the *National Conference on Yoga and Indian Approaches to Psychology* held in Pondicherry and signed by 160 researchers (retrieved January 16, 2018, from www.ipi.org.in/texts/yaiap/pondicherrymanifesto.php). Here, Indian psychology was described as "[a] Western transplant, unable to connect with the Indian ethos and concurrent community conditions." The manifesto argued that because of this, Indian psychology had been ineffective in supporting India's national development.

Indian IP developed in different directions. These were reduced to two by Sundararajan, Misra, and Marsella (2013), the first of which was described as "indigenization of Western psychology (Sinha, 1997, p. 70)". This direction can thus be seen as *indigenization from without*. Examples are studies on Indian versions of leadership (e.g., J. B. P. Sinha) and studies on positive thinking and well-being. The second direction turned to concepts in traditional religious writing and tried to explicate them in more modern terms. This approach was described by Sundararajan et al. (2013) as focusing on Indian traditional thought and as reconstructing classical ideas by means of indigenous intellectual resources. These efforts also included attempts to integrate Western psychology and Indian thinking. Misra and Paranjpe (2012, p. 883) described this direction as a kind of integration of traditional and modern thinking. Finally, J. B. P. Sinha (in Allwood & Berry, 2006, p. 256) described this approach (or a version of this approach) as "a trend towards de-colonization of psychological knowledge by searching the philosophical roots of Indian wisdom and retrieving indigenous concepts and psychological processes from the ancient texts." These concepts were sometimes empirically operationalized and explored by modern mainstream research methods, and were often simply described.

In general, Indian IP has tended to have an open attitude to interdisciplinary and international contacts (Sinha, 1993). One reason for this may again be India's colonial past, which has had a deep impact on India, for example with respect to the prevalence of English in Indian academia. Sharma (2015, p. 189) asked if an Indian identity could be defined without including "Western languages, education, methods and cultural import?" This may be one reason why much of Indian IP has had a somewhat soft approach to indigenization, simply using conventional research methods to test the need to modify Western-originated concepts and methods in the Indian context.

There has been some critique of IP in India. Adair (e.g., 1998, p. 23) argued that Indian IP, and other IPs, should not delve deeply into traditional concepts since this risks getting lost in esotericism and thereby limiting practical usability. Thus, Adair (1998) put limited value on indigenous cultural anchoring per se and argued that such an approach had diminished the contribution of Indian IP to the country's national development.

A critical note on a somewhat different line, illustrating the distinction between the first and the second meaning of the term "indigenous psychology" as discussed in the Introduction, is Sinha's (1993, p. 34, italics in original) warning that "[i]ndigenization is not to be confused with the revivalism that has been in evidence since independence and is often known as *Indian psychology.*" Here *Indian psychology* is taken to be psychology that does not separate clearly between religion and science.

With respect to the future of Indian IP, Poortinga (2016) noted that, in terms of numbers of psychologists and students, and volume of research, psychology in India has grown in recent decades. However, Adair et al. (2009) found that, although psychology in India had been very successful in the 1980s with respect to publication and visibility in the international arena, in recent years it has shown a declining rate of international publication. Adair et al. suggested different reasons for this, such as changes in higher education, retirements, and the possibility that psychology had become less attractive as a career. In addition, Misra and Paranjpe (2012) observed that despite the fact that there is some tendency in Indian psychology to leave Western psychology behind and move toward an increased use of an IP approach, Western psychological models and theories are still used and tested in India. Moreover, theoretical developments "such as feminism, subaltern studies, critical theory, and post modernism are providing new ways of engaging with reality" (p. 890). The same authors also observed a general shift in Indian IP toward using "qualitative approaches."

J. B. P. Sinha (in Allwood & Berry, 2006, p. 256) ended his description of Indian IP by noting that "indigenous psychology is still a 'little culture' dominated by Western psychology." Similarly, Misra and Paranjpe (2012, p. 885) noted that "[w]hile culturally informed studies are on the rise, full scale reconceptualization or indigenous theorization has been limited." In general, the size of IP in India is not clear, partly because, as pointed out by Sinha (e.g., 1993, 1997), indigenization comes in degrees and different kinds.

2.6 Indigenization in Muslim Countries

The indigenization of psychology in countries such as Pakistan, Malaysia, and Iran, where Islam is an important factor, has to a large extent been influenced by this religion. As described by Long (2014), the need to Islamicize psychology received attention at about the same time as the need for indigenization of psychology was noticed in other parts of the world, and the observed reasons for this were similar. That is, the psychology developed in the West did not fit the social realities in Muslim countries; in particular, it did not fit well with the teachings of Islam.

The well-known book *The dilemma of Muslim psychologists* by Malik Badri (1979) describes the shortcomings of modern psychology and is a good illustration of this discontent. In this book Badri, from the standpoint of Islamic psychology, observed that the personality, motivation, and behavior theories of Western psychology contradict Islam in many ways. As Badri summarized (p. 103):

> We have criticized the major schools of western psychology, like behaviorism and psychoanalysis, in terms of their inability to deal with deep Islamic psychospiritual phenomena. In one way or the other, these schools are greatly influenced by atheistic positivist philosophy, they may have a pessimistic or distorted concept of human nature, and are either too simplistic or too biased to explain and entertain religious and spiritual processes.

Attempts to Islamicize psychology are sometimes part of a broader approach called Islamic science. Furlow (1996, p. 262) argued that the interest in the Islamization of knowledge was a product of "a perceived crisis within the Islamic civilization," and he described three directions in the contemporary development of Islamization of knowledge: modernization, indigenization and nativization. The modernists argue that "science is value-free, neutral and objective" (p. 263) and that such a science historically has been part of the Islamic tradition.

The indigenization camp argues against the separation between a rational, scientific approach to knowledge and an Islamic approach. Instead, the two should be reunified – that is, a scientific approach should be integrated with an Islamic religious approach. Furlow classified the project to develop Islamicized knowledge, as formulated by, e.g., *The International Institute of Islamic Thought* (Sulayman, 1989), as falling under the indigenization direction. In this attempt the principle of "Tahwid," *unity*, is emphasized. This means, for example, that science and Islam will not deliver separate conclusions. Sulayman (1989) spelled out the approach to Islamic thought and postulated that "mankind has been given free will" (p. 34). Kuala Lumpur's *International*

Islamic University Malaysia (IIUM) took an active early role in the
Islamization of knowledge project (Long, 2014). Badri, originally from
Sudan, joined the faculty of IIUM's department of psychology in 1992,
where he was the first to give a course on Islam and psychology for under-
graduate students.

Finally, the nativization approach, as rendered by Furlow (1996), argues that
the worldview of modernist science is different and that it therefore is not
helpful when it comes to solving problems in Islamic societies. As a consequence, an authentic Islamic science should be developed. Such a science
should be built on "an Islamic *epistemological* foundation" (1996, p. 267,
italics in original). A debate exists about how such a science should be
constructed; for example, Huff (1996) and Inayatullah (1996) discussed different forms of Islamic science. In brief, the division between religion and science
is often not clear in Islamic science. For example, by prioritizing the truth of the
Koran and the principle of unity, *Tahwid*, in Islamic science, Ghamari-Tabrizi
(1996) arrived at the conclusion that if results from scientific research contradict the Koran, then science is wrong.

Two general forms of Islamicizing psychology have developed (Long,
2014). Long described one of these, the "revisionist camp," as "a critical
revision of Western psychology – involving the exegesis of relevant pas-
sages from the Qur'an" (p. 16) – that is, *indigenization from without*. The
other form, the "classical camp," is described as elaborating the classical
Islamic tradition (Long, 2014) – that is, *indigenization from within*. Long
noted that a "theocentric-individualistic outlook" characterizes both versions. For example, according to Noor, writing in the revisionist camp in
2009 (reviewed by Long, 2014), the approach does not reject Western
psychology, but it re-examines Western knowledge so that it coheres with
Islamic teachings. In the next section, I describe IP in Iran as an illustration
of IP in a Muslim country.

2.6.1 Iran

The indigenization of psychology in Iran had a definite start in 1978 with
Khomeini's theocratic revolution against the Shah and his dependence on the
West (Moghaddam, in Allwood & Berry, 2006). Moghaddam noted that "[t]he
attack on the Shah was associated with an attack on Western world-views,
particularly in psychology and economics" (p. 257). Furthermore, the state put
a generalized pressure on psychologists to give up Western models and to
develop a psychology that fitted the Iranian reality. Given that many people in
Iran were enthusiastic about the revolution in the beginning, this decree may

have been in line with sentiments at the population level (see, e.g., Ebadi, 2006).

Three different movements in IP in Iran were identified by Moghaddam (in Allwood & Berry, 2006). The first aims to develop an "Islamic psychology" and has been ongoing since the early 1970s. Its authors mainly write in Farsi, not in English, and it is supported by the Iranian state. An example of a research topic of this kind, noted by Thorngate (2008) is "prayer." Moghaddam described this version as showing "ideological leanings and lack of attention to empirical research," and as not receiving much attention in prominent psychology departments. The second and third versions of IP described by Moghaddam are research on gender and on "democracy and social change." These versions are often seen as "being associated with movements opposed to the Islamic government" (in Allwood & Berry, 2006, p. 257). This has resulted in the government's censors disallowing publication of research produced by these versions. Such governmental resentment may also be due to factors similar to those identified by Tohidi (2016) as affecting the feminist movement in Iran. This movement is described as mainly made up of the middle class in big cities, and as a consequence of modernity and of industrial capitalism. Furthermore, Tohidi argued that, due to being associated with Western domination, the movement has come under suspicion by its enemies. In brief, the development of IP in Iran appears to be heavily dependent on specific ensuing political conflicts and developments in Iran.

IP appears to be fairly limited in Iran. Moghaddam (in Allwood & Berry, 2006) noted that in 2005 there was still an interest in IP, but that the use of US psychology in particular was considerable. This was described to clearly be the case "in the most competitive universities, where professors with the highest status are those with the greatest success in working with traditional Western models of psychology" (p. 257). Thorngate (2008) observed that 80% or more of Iranian psychological research is limited to the use of correlations. Furthermore, it tends to study individual differences by means of Western questionnaires translated into Farsi. Interestingly, Thorngate (2008) also reported that around 2006 the Iranian government began to encourage researchers to publish more in international journals, especially those listed by the *Institute for Scientific Information* (ISA).

2.7 Africa

In many countries in Africa psychology is not well developed. In 1993 there were only fourteen departments of psychology located in ten African countries, five of them in Nigeria (Durojaiye, 1993). Research funding is mostly provided from outside of the country, which makes it difficult to procure means for research related to African social issues (Oppong, 2016). Mayer (2002, p. 4) noted that "the publishing industry in Africa is still in its infancy and consequently editors are overburdened with work" (see also Durojaiye, 1993). She also noted that African psychologists are said to experience difficulties in publishing their work internationally.

Despite the low level of development of psychology in Africa, some calls for the need to indigenize psychology occurred early on. For example, Abdi (1975) noted that Western psychology is foreign to African thinking. However, in 1996 Eze (reviewed in Mayer, 2002) observed that African psychological research tends to use theories from Western psychology, but that the results from this research have not influenced theoretical formulations. In line with this Mayer concluded that psychology in Africa is influenced by Western psychology, but the reverse is not the case. However, it is encouraging that from 2006 *The Journal of Psychology in Africa* established a platform on the Internet (that year as volume 16). The journal appears to be partly operated from the USA and, in addition, South Africa, Nigeria, and a few other countries seem to be the most active partners. On its homepage, under "Aims and Scope," the journal notes that "[i]ts core mission is to advance psychological research for the social-cultural and health development in Africanist settings, inclusive of the African diaspora communities around the globe. Research that addresses African heritage realities and opportunities is particularly encouraged."

Africa is, generally speaking, a very diverse continent. To illustrate with the countries described below, Cameroon has a population of about 24 million people (June, 2018, according to the Worldometers on the net: www.worldometers.info/world-population/, retrieved 29 June, 2018) and has approximately 250 ethnic groups. Nigeria has more than 195 million inhabitants (June, 2018; Worldometers, link as previously) and approximately 200 ethnic groups. Showing somewhat less diversity, Ghana has a population of approximately 29 million (January, 2018; Worldometers, link as previously) with about eight ethnic groups with more than 1% of the population in Ghana. Thus, the task of indigenizing psychology at a specific ethnic level in Africa would be a very challenging task. However, Sections 2.7.1–2.7.3 provide descriptions of the state of indigenization of psychology in some African countries.

2.7.1 Cameroon

Nsamenang (2013) noted that, currently, there are few academic psychologists working in Cameroon, compared to other African states such as

Ghana, Nigeria, and South Africa. He also described a tension between psychological researchers who write in French and those who write in English due to earlier differences in colonial influences on the discipline. Although the *Cameroon Psychological Society* was founded in 1987, it has seen little activity, and a new society, *The Cameroon Anglophone Psychological Association*, was created in 2012 in order to increase activity. Bame Nsamenang, at the University of Bamenda, is a leading figure for IP in Cameroon. He has a broad research profile, covering, among other things, developmental lifespan psychology, and he works to integrate "African knowledge" into international research on human development and education. Despite the above-described situation, Nsamenang and colleagues have been very active. This is illustrated by the large *Handbook of African Education Theories and Practices* he edited with Therese Tchombe, which was published in 2011. Nsamenang (in Allwood & Berry, 2006, p. 259) noted two trends in Cameroon IP: the first is to "free education/training curricula from excessive Eurocentrism" including training of "professionals and scholars ... including psychologists." The second trend is for developmental research "to focus on African social ontogeny, a developmental path in lifespan perspective within an African world-view, espoused by Nsamenang (1992, 2001)."

2.7.2 Ghana

Oppong (2016) reported on psychology and indigenization of psychology in Ghana and elsewhere in Africa. The University of Ghana was the first, between 1963–1967, to establish a department of psychology in Ghana. This department continues to play a leading role in the development of psychology in Ghana, and it is the only one that offers a PhD in psychology (Asante & Oppong, 2012; however, the University of Cape Coast offers a PhD training program in curriculum and teaching). In general, psychology in Ghana has tended to have an applied orientation, for example in education, police work, and health care work, and this makes the issue of indigenizing psychology very relevant. Furthermore, the only journal that seems directly associated with psychological research in Ghana, *The Ghana Journal of Psychology*, seems to currently be inactive. Moreover, psychological research in Ghana tends to use survey methodology.

Oppong (2016) argued that a problem facing Ghana is that the psychological research taught and applied there can be seen as a weaker form of Western psychology, and the Ghanaian folk psychology that is attended to in the context of research psychology is trivialized due to lack of contact with the everyday population in Ghana. Here Moghaddam and Taylor's (1985) observation about the concurrent presence of dual sectors, one modern and one traditional, in developing countries is worthy of consideration. Such a split is likely to decrease the effectiveness of the social work based on research results produced by modern researchers. However, Oppong still argued that psychology has contributed to national development in, for example, the education and industry sectors (e.g., personnel selection). At the same time the fact that Asante and Oppong (2012) described the lack of involvement of the state in the development of psychology in Ghana and that they encouraged Ghanaian students to study psychology abroad are clear signs of the deficient general autochthonization of psychology in Ghana.

The IP supported by Oppong (2016) is a milder form of IP than that promoted, for example, in the Philippines (SP). For example, he suggested that Western psychological concepts should not be totally rejected, but instead could serve as a breeding ground for new ideas. As he puts it, the challenge is how to Westernize and still keep what is worth preserving of Ghanaian ideas. Thus, he advised that the psychological curriculum should include compulsory courses on African philosophical and psychological thought, traditional proverbs, courses relating to the history and social anthropology of Ghana, and (though it is not clear why) a course on parapsychology. Asante and Oppong (2012) recommended the book, *African cultural values: An introduction*, published in 1996, written by Gyekye, a Ghanaian philosopher, and *Tradition and change in Ghana: An introduction to sociology*, published in 2003 by Nukunya, as aids in developing a Ghanaian approach to psychology.

In this context Oppong (2016, p. 9) wrote that "[i]ntroduction of such courses should encourage Ghanaian psychologists [to] explore Ghanaian ethnic cosmologies to identify and describe their cognitive, affective, and behavioral processes and content in order to elevate folk and philosophical Ghanaian psychologies to indigenous scientific psychology." A further commentator on psychology in Ghana, Mate-Kole (2013), suggested that, in line with traditional Ghanaian beliefs, studies should also include research into the effects of the day of the week on which a person is born. In similarity to most IPs, Asante and Oppong (2012) recommended research on social issues relevant to the current Ghanaian society. Interestingly enough, in a long list of such issues, the authors mentioned "outmoded cultural practices" (p. 475). The same authors also argued for the use of a combination of qualitative and quantitative methods, and for the use of exploratory research.

Oppong (2016) warned against the proliferation of IPs in Africa. The reason for his warning was that such IPs were likely to be based on national borders created by Western powers at the Berlin conference of 1885 and would therefore be unproductive. In this context Oppong pointed to Western psychology, as developed in the singular, as a good example. In line with this, he also suggested that a Pan-African psychology should be identified. He defined it as "*a branch of psychology where the population of interest is persons of African origin, and/or where the target population resides either on the continent of Africa or in the Diaspora*" (2016, p. 10, italics in original).

As a start, Oppong (2016, p. 10) differentiated among four target populations for Pan-African psychology. These are classed as a combination of two dimensions: 1) "Africans of the soil"/"African by blood," encompassing Sub-Saharan Africans; 2) "Africans of the soil"/"African not by blood," encompassing North Africans; 3) "Africans not of the soil"/"African by blood," encompassing "African Americans, Afro-Caribbeans, and Mulattos"; and, finally, 4) "Africans not of the soil"/"African not by blood," encompassing "Africans through adoption, marriage, acquired citizenship, and shared lived experience." To justify these groups, Oppong (2016, p. 10) noted that "[t]hus, Pan-African psychology is an indigenous psychology in which both Africans of the soil and by blood are the target population due to their shared history, conditions of living, values, and traditions." Oppong also argued that group (4) is interesting since "their inclusion is key to a comprehensive appreciation of human behaviour within such a discipline. By their association with Africans, such persons take on a new form of personshood [*sic*] that is neither Western nor African. As a result, one cannot administer Western nor African interventions to such persons without appropriate adaptations or modifications" (p. 10). It seems that what Oppong is looking for here is the development of research on what is common to all persons with almost any kind of connection to Africa. Mate-Kole (2013) mentioned "spirituality" as a possible example of such a common feature of all Africans, or at least of *the African*.

2.7.3 Nigeria

The first psychology department in Nigeria was founded about 1964 in Nsukka, and around the year 2000 Nigeria was one of the countries in Africa with the most psychology departments (Mayer, 2002). Moreover, The University of Lagos was the first in black Africa to offer a psychology course, in 1986/87. Mayer characterized psychology in Nigeria as "problem-oriented," rather than theoretically oriented (p. 2) and provided various indications of the poor development of the psychological research community in Nigeria. Thus, at least around 2000 the indigenization of psychology in Nigeria had apparently not developed very far.

2.8 Australia, New Zealand, and Other Fourth-World IPs

IPs in Australia, New Zealand, and other places have taken on a specific profile that specifically focuses on minority groups, so-called *fourth-world peoples* (e.g., Aboriginal Australians and the Maori of New Zealand). Moreover, these IPs often appear to have been built up by representatives from the very minority groups that they have the ambition to represent. Such IPs have also started to develop in, for example, the USA and Canada (e.g., Tuck, 2013), taking the perspective of Native Americans in the USA and, correspondingly, First Nation Peoples in Canada. These IPs represent a somewhat newer development in the IP movement. Due to its longer legacy, IP in New Zealand will be presented first.

Nikora (in Allwood & Berry, 2006) criticized research on the Maori between 1940–1960 by noting that it was "on" Maori, instead of "with" Maori. According to Nikora, "psychiatrist, psychologist, and professor of Maori Studies, Mason Durie (e.g., 1994)" is "[m]ost central to advancing the Maori development agenda" (p. 255). Durie emphasized that "a secure Maori identity correlates with good health and wellness" (Nikora, 2007, p. 82). (Note: Nikora, 2007, appears to spell Durie as "Dude"). Although efforts to indigenize had started earlier, in a report from 1987 Abbott and Durie argued that psychology was the most monocultural of the professional training programs they had encountered (Nikora, in Allwood & Berry, 2006). This report and other early work was an important impetus to further indigenization in New Zealand.

Linda Waimarie Nikora is professor of Indigenous Studies at Te Wānanga o Waipapa, University of Auckland, and is a leading researcher in the New Zealand context. Her research has focused on various aspects of the Maori, including Maori identity, well-being, and way of life. As described by Nikora (in Allwood & Berry, 2006, p. 254), IP in Australia and New Zealand is engaged in studies of "the Maori term tikanga, or customary practice – those behaviours, values, ways of doing things, and understanding actions that have always and will continue to be with us."

Maori IP has a clearly applied perspective. It aims to create a psychology that can help Maori people and also keep their cultural heritage. Such a psychology would make "for a better collective Maori future. It is a journey towards Maori self-determination" (Nikora, in Allwood & Berry, 2006, p. 255; see also Nikora, 2007). Later on the same page, Nikora modestly concluded that "[a]lthough a slow process, there is a small yet active group of people who are making a contribution through practice, teaching, research, or involvement in professional organizations." Nikora (2007) further described the systematic work done to build up the autochthonization of Maori IP.

Pat Dudgeon, professor at the School of Indigenous Studies, University of Western Australia (UWA), is a leading researcher in the Australian context. Dudgeon is a psychologist and was the first Aboriginal (from the Bardi people of the Kimberley) to take a PhD exam. The School of Indigenous Studies at UWA declares its aim as "to achieve excellence and equity in all aspects of higher education for Aboriginal and Torres Strait Islander people" (www.sis .uwa.edu.au/, retrieved June 28, 2018). Dudgeon is currently chair of the *Indigenous Australian Psychologists Association.* Her home page biography at the Australian Indigenous Psychologists Association (www.indigenouspsy chology.com.au/profiles/187/professor-pat-dudgeon, retrieved June 28, 2018) states that she "is actively involved with the Aboriginal community and has a commitment to social justice for Indigenous people." She has carried out research on many topics – for example, issues relating to identity and health among Aboriginal peoples in Australia, including community research on interventions to improve mental health among the same groups (see, e.g., Dudgeon et al., 2017, and other papers in that special issue).

Fourth-world IPs in Australia, New Zealand, and North America currently appear to be active and vibrant. This may have to do with their clearly applied perspective and with the fact that historically, and to some extent continuing, oppression by primarily whites has been so obvious. Moreover, as described by various authors (e.g., Tuck, 2013), researchers from the majority society have commonly been seen as oppressors among these groups. This has been the case also among other minority groups (e.g., the Sami people, an indigenous Finno-Ugric minority people living in the north of Scandinavia and Russia). In this context, Tuck (2013) cited the methodology book *Decolonializing methodologies: Research and indigenous peoples* by L. T. Smith (published in its second edition, 2012): "research has a huge credibility problem in the Indigenous world" (p. 122); "[i]t is relentlessly ideological, yet it has the power to distort, to make invisible, to overlook, to exaggerate" (p. 367). It is also interesting that some of these ethnic groups, both in the Australia/New Zealand area and in North America, have started to take control of what work researchers will be allowed to carry out involving the group in question (see, e.g., Tuck, 2013).

The journal *AlterNative: An International Journal of Indigenous Peoples,* was founded in 2005 and aims "to present scholarly research on Indigenous worldviews and experiences of decolonization from Indigenous perspectives from around the world" (from journal homepage, www.alternative.ac.nz/con tent/alternative-journal, retrieved January 2018). In line with these developments, Dudgeon (2017) concluded that in recent decades psychology has shifted from viewing indigenous people as objects to be researched to seeing them as agents who create meaning and change. This approach allows for action research and other forms of active involvement in research by the participants in IP research.

2.9 Latin America

Psychology in Latin America to some extent has its own character. Cultural-social, experimental, cognitive, and psychoanalytic (the last, especially in Argentina) approaches are prevalent, as is emphasis on the application of these (Diaz-Loving, 2005; Sanzez Sosa & Valderrama-Iturbe, 2001; Torres & Consoli, 2015). Although many kinds of psychological research are carried out, a broad, fairly holistic, social psychological approach with a sociological cultural twist is typical. Two well-known examples are action-oriented liberation psychology and the Mexican ethnopsychological approach (including the holistic, so-called *historic biopsychosocial* model). The ethnopsychological approach is commonly counted as an IP approach and originates from Rogelio Diaz-Guerrero, often seen as a pioneer of Latin American IP (Diaz-Guerrero, 1993; Diaz-Loving, 2015). As applied in Mexico, this approach aims to describe the Mexican individual and his/her personality.

Adair (2006) argued that there is a smaller need for indigenization of psychology in Latin America than in, for example, Asia. In line with this, it also seems that the activity in IPs is noticeably greater in East and South Asia compared to Latin America. Of the countries in Latin America, Mexico stands out as an important bastion of IP, and in Mexico, the National University of Mexico. Here Diaz-Guerrero and Ronaldo Diaz-Loving have been important actors.

2.10 North America: Canada

As recounted by John Berry (in Allwood & Berry, 2006), in the 1970s Canada experienced a wave of "emergent nationalism" which many academics saw as being anti-American. In this context Berry and Wilde, in a book published in1972, argued that social psychology in Canada was imitative of US social psychology. Similarly, Adair (1999, p. 412) described the situation in Canada, before the development of Canadian IP, as follows: "We adapted their [the US] code of Ethics as our own, and our departments sought APA clinical program accreditation. However, Canada is an independent country. Canadian psychology had to develop and take on its own identity." The Canadian IP movement argued that psychology instead should be rooted in the specific features of Canadian social reality. Such features, noted by Berry (in Allwood & Berry,

2006, p. 260), are "living in the north; understanding both English–French, and Aboriginal–non-Aboriginal relations; and researching multiculturalism." Berry also recorded that most Canadian psychologists did not participate in the initiative toward Canadian IP and often saw it as anti-American, whereas the promotors of Canadian IP saw it as non-American. In contrast to psychology *in* Canada (i.e., an imposed etic), Berry and others wanted to promote a psychology *of* Canada. This psychology would start from the local context and take an "emic" perspective. As suggested by Berry, this research was to be applied to four psychological domains: social, clinical, educational, and work psychology.

Adair (1999) noted that, although great financial resources were deployed, it took twenty years to develop an IP in Canada. For Adair, developing an IP meant achieving an *autochthonous* psychology. This development, as described by Adair, included as the first step "clos[ing] the door to any more imported faculty. 'Canadian First' was the instruction to all hiring committees" (p. 413).

It is not quite clear what status Canadian IP (CIP) has today. In November 2017, the homepage of the Canadian Psychological Association showed that among thirty-two sections there are just three that seem related to CIP: the sections for Aboriginal psychology, community psychology, and international and cross-cultural psychology, but none of these mention IP directly. Similarly, in his presidential address to the Canadian Psychological Association, Thomas Hadjistavropoulos (2009) described the distinctiveness of Canadian psychology. This purported distinctiveness included influence of both Anglophone (UK and US; theory and methods) and Francophone (France; applied orientation) psychology, establishment of the first *First Nations University* (FNU) in Canada, and an Aboriginal Psychology section within the Canadian Psychological Association. The FNU, according to its homepage (http://fnu niv.ca/overview, retrieved November 2017), "is a unique Canadian institution that specializes in Indigenous knowledge, providing post-secondary education for Indigenous and non-Indigenous students alike within a culturally supportive environment." When describing his year of presidency, Hadjistavropoulos noted that he had encouraged Aboriginal issues, but he did not mention the term "indigenous psychology" in his address.

3 International Level of IP

As described above, the development of IPs has occurred in interaction with Western psychology and Western psychologists, both with respect to practical support and with respect to theoretical conceptualizations. At the same time, IP researchers' interactions with non-Western psychologists are also likely to have been important. Many Western psychologists played an important role in the early phases, helping to build up psychology in non-Western contexts. With respect to practical support, many of the early cross-cultural psychologists, such as Robert Serpell (Zambia) and Gustav Jahoda (Ghana, see e.g., Durojaiye, 1993) helped in the establishment of psychology departments.

An important factor at the international level for the development of IPs was the development of cross-cultural psychology in the 1960s and 1970s. The organizational development associated with cross-cultural psychology is well described by Lonner (2013), who early on played an important role in this development. Researchers with an interest in cross-cultural psychology started to organize themselves at a number of international conferences, for example, in 1958 in Bangkok, 1967 in Ibadan, Nigeria, and in 1971 in Istanbul, Turkey. This development culminated with the founding of the IACCP in 1972 at a conference in Hong Kong. In January 2018, the homepage of the IACCP (www.iaccp.org/node/1) stated that the IACCP had more than 800 members from more than sixty-five countries.

Cross-cultural psychology tests the validity of universal claims made by mainstream psychology. Berry (1997, p. 140) defined cross-cultural psychology as aiming "to account for individual and group differences in psychological characteristics as a function of population-level factors," and noted that both "cultural" and "comparative" are suitable descriptions for cross-cultural psychologists. Among the researchers listed by Lonner (2013) as having made important early contributions to the development of cross-cultural psychology are Robert Serpell, Herman Witkin, Harry Triandis, and John Berry.

With respect to IP more specifically, the role of international organizations such as *The International Union of Psychological Science* (IUPsyS; established in 1951), and especially the IACCP, should be emphasized. Many of the pioneers of IP, such as Berry, Ho, Loving-Diaz, Pandey, D. Sinha, and J. D. P. Sinha, have been members of the board of the IACCP. Thus, as described, for example, for the case of India by J. D. P Sinha (in Allwood & Berry, 2006, p. 256), "[f]ormation of the IACCP certainly provided a rallying ground for psychologists from non-Western cultures to think of alternative psychologies. Collaboration with some of the Western psychologists (e.g., John Berry, Harry Triandis, among others) facilitated the process."

In addition, meeting other IP researchers at various symposia at different conferences, such as the conferences of the *IACCP* and the *International Association of Applied Psychology* (IAAP), is likely to have influenced the development of IPs. The IUPsyS also arranged and sponsored symposia at different large international conferences. In Asia, the *Asian Association for Social Psychology* (AASP; founded in 1995) has been very active in promoting research relating to IP. Kim (1995) described the goal of the AASP as to promote the contribution of Asian psychologists by helping to integrate the rich Asian cultural heritages with psychology. And, as stated on the AASP homepage, (https://asiansocialpsych.org/, retrieved February 7, 2018), "[the organization] promotes research on Asian traditions, philosophies, and ideas that have scientific merit and practical applications, and expands the boundary, substance, and direction of social psychology by supplementing and integrating Western psychology's focus on intra-individual processes with a broader and more holistic view from culture and society." Since 1995, the association has organized bi-annual conferences, and it has published the *Asian Journal of Social Psychology* since 1998.

In 2010 a further notable development occurred in Asia when the society *The Asian Association of Indigenous and Cultural Psychology* (AAICP) was founded in connection with The *First Conference of Indigenous and Cultural Psychology* at Universitas Gadjah Mada, Yogyakarta, Indonesia. K.-K. Hwang was elected as the first president of the association. Other active researchers in the organization are U. Kim, G. Mishra, S. Yamaguchi, K. W. Yuniarti, M. A. Faturochman, S. Subandi and A. Supratiknya (the latter four of whom are from Indonesia). Since 2010, the organization has organized yearly international conferences on IP.

The same year (2010) also saw the founding of the *Center for Indigenous and Cultural Psychology* at the same university, Universitas Gadjah Mada. Members of the advisory committee for this center are to a large extent the same researchers who participated in the founding of the AAICP. The Vision and Mission section of the center's homepage (http://cicp.psikologi.ugm.ac .id/ENG/?page_id=86, retrieved March 7, 2018). proclaims that the center is "a leading academic organization dedicated to advancing and facilitating research in the field of indigenous and cultural psychology," and that it aims "[t]o become the first formal institution in accommodating the development of indigenous and cultural psychology. To strengthen the position of indigenous and cultural psychology through continuing scientific support [and] To construct psychological concepts from social and cultural context" The page also announces that the center "revolves around constructive realism ... [and] emphasizes the utmost importance of translating social discourse according to its context in order to avoid homogenized thinking." (http://cicp.psikologi.ugm.ac.id/ENG/?page_id=17, retrieved March 7, 2018).

In 2010 a further IP-relevant event occurred, namely the formation of the APA-based *Indigenous Psychology Task Force* (under Division 32, Society for Humanistic Psychology), with Louise Sundararajan as chairperson. In January 2018 the task force had about 180 members. The APA homepage for the task force (www.apadivisions.org/division-32/leadership/task-forces/indigenous/index.aspx retrieved June 29, 2018) declares that IP is

> based on the following factors: 1. A reaction against the colonization/hegemony of Western psychology. 2. The need for non-Western cultures to solve their local problems through indigenous practices and applications. 3. The need for a non-Western culture to recognize itself in the constructs and practices of psychology. 4. The need to use indigenous philosophies and concepts to generate theories of global discourse.

Next, developments in the international English-language literature about the theoretical basis of IPs carried out by IP authors are described. An early contribution to this literature was an anthology on IP: *Indigenous psychologies: Research and experience in cultural context*, edited by Kim and Berry (1993b). This book has become something of a classic in the field, and it includes chapters by many of the pioneers of IP, such as R. Diaz-Guerrero, V. Enriquez, D. Y.-F. Ho, F. M. Moghaddam, and D. Sinha. Other important anthologies with work by IP researchers are volumes edited by Kao and Sinha (1997); Kim, Yang, and Hwang (2006a); and Misra and Mohanty (2002). There have also been a number of special issues on IP in journals such as *Applied Psychology: An International Review*, the *Asian Journal of Social Psychology*, and the *International Journal of Psychology*.

One much-debated question concerns the relationship between IPs and other related types of psychology. This question has received different answers from various IP researchers. Early on, many IP researchers aligned themselves with cross-cultural psychology. For example, Kim and Berry (1993a) asserted that cross-cultural psychology is closest to IP. They further argued that the IP approach stands for indigenization "from within," and cross-cultural psychology stands for indigenization "from without." They also remarked that the two approaches are complementary and not mutually exclusive. Likewise, Ho (1998, p. 101) wrote that "indigenous psychologies are best seen as a subdomain of cross-cultural psychology," and Sinha (2002, p. 23) similarly saw the approaches as complementary, stating that "I have definitional difficulty in distinguishing between ethnopsychology, folk psychology, psychological anthropology, cultural psychology, societal psychology and indigenous psychology." A related view was asserted more recently by Poortinga (2016, p. 162): "an indigenous psychology is based on cross-cultural differences, that is, local behavioral manifestations found somewhere that differ from manifestations found elsewhere."

However, during the 2000s other IP authors declared an affinity to *cultural psychology*, an approach pioneered by Michael Cole (1996) and Richard Shweder (1990). These authors criticized what they found to be the abstract comparative approach of cross-cultural psychology. Cole has promoted an approach based on the Soviet cultural-historical school, where the activities carried out by people in their everyday life (e.g., in their work to support themselves) are what shape their cognitive skills and other mental properties. Richard Shweder (see, e.g., 1990) has a background that encompasses both psychology and social anthropology, and takes an interactive context-sensitive, multidisciplinary approach. Thus, he has forcefully argued against the postulate of what he called the *Platonic central processing mechanism*, which basically assumes that people operate in context-free environments. In addition, Shweder has argued that people operate in *local intentional worlds* where they strive to reach their goals. This is also the type of theoretical framework he recommends for cultural psychological studies. Furthermore, he argued that psyche and culture are related by means of intention and causality: "Intentional things are causally active, but only by virtue of our mental representations of them" (1990, p. 2).

IP authors who have aligned themselves with cultural psychology and distanced themselves from cross-cultural psychology have often represented East Asian IPs (see e.g., Kim et al., 2000; Kim, Yang, & Hwang, 2006b). But other authors have also concurred (e.g., Padalia, 2017). In line with this, Shweder (2000, p. 221) concluded that there is little difference between cultural psychology and IP; they "are on exactly the same page," with the important caveat that some cultural understanding should be seen as shared between societies.

Both cross-cultural and cultural psychology are continuously changing and expanding, and both are developing sub-schools. Thus, for example, Poortinga (2016, p. 169) claimed that developments in "cultural psychology [have] moved away from Shweder's (1990, 1991) position towards the traditional comparative paradigm of cross-cultural psychology and its universalist logic." In general, Poortinga associated Shweder's cultural psychology with relativist thinking and argued that "relativist thinking in cultural psychology as antithetical to universalist ideas in the culture-comparative tradition is a position that is being left behind" (p. 169).

However, this may be somewhat of a simplification. Lonner (2013) observed that many researchers are primarily interested in "culture" and that they often identify with many directions in culture-oriented psychology. He noted that about one-third of the members of the IACCP in a recent survey reported viewing themselves both as cross-cultural psychologists and as cultural psychologists. In brief, irrespective of labeling and approaches, it is fair to say that North American psychologists such as Albert Bandura, John Berry, Kenneth Gergen, and Richard Shweder have had a great influence on IPs with respect to conceptualizations, theories, and frameworks. Such influence might be seen as part of indigenization from without.

4 Challenges

As noted, IPs are changing, and along the way they face a number of possible challenges. Some of these are discussed in this section. This part of the Element has more the character of a debate contribution, and my aim is mostly to inspire discussion about the issues. There may not always be simple solutions, and I obviously do not claim to provide complete solutions to any of the issues, although it will often be clear in which direction I lean.

4.1 Meaning of Indigenization and Indigenous Psychology

IP writers differ in their views about what indigenization means and what IPs are, and it is fair to say that the notion of IP to some extent has functioned as a creative *generative concept* allowing different authors in the IP community to describe their own preferred form of IP. We now take a brief look at ideas about the nature of IPs offered by some of the more active IP researchers.

In a classic definition of IP, Kim and Berry (1993a, p. 2) defined the discipline as "the scientific study of human behavior (or the mind) that is native, that is not transported from other regions, and that is designed for its people." A further definition that has been accepted by many IP researchers is the one by Ho (1998). Ho defined IP as "the study of human behavior and mental processes within a cultural context that relies on values, concepts, belief systems, methodologies, and other resources indigenous to the specific ethnic or cultural group under investigation; these indigenous resources may be applied to different points in the entire process by which psychological knowledge is generated" (p. 94). Both of these definitions are unclear with respect to whether all, or just some, of the components of IP research should come from the IP researcher's own culture, and as illustrated earlier, the views on this matter differ.

Yang (2012), somewhat abstractly, characterized IP (which he abbreviates as IZP) as something that "explores the rationales and methods that are most effective for conducting indigenized research in non-Western countries" (p.

25). He also noted that *indigenized research* is "research in which indigenous-minded non-Western psychologists try to re-root their theoretical, methodological, and empirical accomplishments into their own native culture through a quasi-emic approach" (p. 14). In the same paper, he noted that IP (IZP) is both a discipline and a methodology. He described the goal of IPs in East Asia more broadly as being to create a local IP that would replace the Westernized psychology in that society. Yang (2012) also argued that the prime purpose of such IPs is to create knowledge and methods that can help in understanding the minds of local people in the sense that they can mirror their minds and be useful for explaining and predicting them. In this way, the knowledge will be useful for solving local personal and social problems. However, since indigenization, according to Yang (2012), can only succeed partially it will not be totally successful in helping to solve such problems.

With respect to methods, Yang (2012) took a method-liberal approach, ostensibly taking his inspiration from qualitative methods as presented by Guba and Lincoln (1994). He argued for a multiple paradigm approach in IP, in that IPs "should adopt ontologically, epistemologically, and methodologically different or even conflicting paradigms like positivism, postpositivism, critical theory (and related positions), and constructionism, as delineated by Guba and Lincoln (1994)" (Yang, 2012, p. 20).

Some characterizations of IP relate to what the *focus* of IPs should be. Enriquez (1977) seemed to suggest that research on personality and national personality is the prime task, or at least one of the main tasks, for Filipino IP. Others concur, to a greater or lesser extent. For example, Ho (1998) asserted that the most important aspect of IPs is that they contribute to the study of personality in mainstream psychology. However, personality theory can mean different things. Ho was not interested in a trait theory of personality. Instead, he argued that a concept of personality that involves a *relational orientation* is suitable not only for IPs, but also for a universal psychology. This approach to personality appears to be a type of trait-situation interaction approach, but one wherein relations are replacing situation.

Other researchers have argued for an IP with more limited ambitions. Adair (1996, p. 51) defined IP as "research that emanates from, adequately represents, and reflects back upon the cultural context in which the behavior is observed." When discussing *complete indigenization*, Adair (e.g., 2006) asked for a complete autochthonization of the discipline in the country, as described earlier, but he did not argue for complete indigenization in the sense of endogeneous indigenization, or indigenization from within.

Instead, he argued for a graded, "monitored" importation of Western psychology, where "there may be much to be gained by recognizing the amount of imported psychology to be retained and the amount to be modified or indigenized" (2006, p. 469). He argued that the need for indigenization depends on the difference between the culture of the IP researcher and US culture, and, in addition, on the general level of development of the psychology discipline in the country. Using this perspective, Adair (2006) concluded that the need for indigenization is "greatest in Asia and Africa, much less in Latin America, even less in Europe and probably least in Canada" (p. 470). Furthermore, Adair (1996) cautioned against spending too much attention on "(a) a narrow search for uniquely native traits or concepts, (b) early religious or philosophical writings, (c) linguistically defined constructs, or less imaginatively, (d) mere identification of differences with Western research findings" (p. 54). In general, Adair (2006), in line with other IP authors such as Kim et al. (1999), emphasized that an IP is successful to the extent that it helps to solve the country's problems – that is, making a practical contribution to the IP researcher's society, also described as contributing to national development.

Relating to the question of what IPs are, Kim and Park (2005) argued that the Canadian IP in the version written about by Adair (e.g., 1999) is not a real IP. The reason was that "the epistemological and scientific paradigm adopted by Canadian psychologists and general psychology is the same" (Kim & Park, 2005, p. 78). In contrast, Adair and Diaz-Loving (1999) argued that the IP developed in Canada *is* an IP because it shows both "increasing cultural sensitivity in concepts, topics and methods; and autochthonisation" (p. 398). It is not clear whether Kim and Park would agree that IP in Canada should be allowed to develop from the grounds of what might be recognized as Canadian culture and, if so, that such Canadian culture might be broadly compatible with the epistemological and scientific paradigm in general psychology. Alternatively, their argument may be that for any aspiring IP to qualify as an IP it has to make a radical break with the prevailing paradigm in general psychology.

Sundararajan, Kim, and Park (2017, p. 2) offered the following somewhat innovative description of IP: "Indigenous psychology represents an alternative scientific paradigm in which the human qualities (e.g., meaning, goals, creativity) and culture have been integrated as central elements of research design." They added that IPs should provide both analytical and phenomenological understanding. For them, this implied that the understanding provided by IP would both be scientific and have relevance for people's everyday life. Their conception of IP showed great ambitions: "Indigenous psychology is needed for all cultural, native, and ethnic groups, including economically developed countries such as Canada, France, and the United States" (Sundararajan et al., 2017, p. 2). However, the authors did not provide much more detail about this. With respect to methods, they reasonably asserted that IPs need not be bound by any methodological commitments.

Sundararajan et al. (2017) also argued that the version of IP spelled out by Kim and Berry in 1993 was not sufficiently theoretically innovative for the needs of cultural psychology. The authors saw such new theoretical grounds for cultural psychology as provided by a new trend they identified in current IPs. Thus, they noted (2017, p. 6) that "[t]his emerging trend in indigenous psychology has two tributaries: One is critical psychology ... the other is study of the indigenous populations."

On the basis of their description of IPs, Sundararajan et al. (2017) noted that in the future, in addition to their practical applied ambitions, IPs will be engaged by "broader social and political issues" (p. 6). This assertion does not seem to recognize that many IPs (though not all; cf. Yang, 2012) have been inherently political from the beginning, both as a general reaction to colonialism and in specific cases such as the *Sikolohiyang Pilipino* (Filipino psychology) promoted by Enriquez (e.g., 1977). Moreover, Sundararajan et al. (2017) envisioned a large research program for IPs in the future: "By exposing the hegemony of Western psychology (De Vos, 2012), and by offering alternatives (Sundararajan, 2013, 2014a, b; Sundararajan and Raina, 2015) in researching the ontological, epistemological, ethical, and spiritual dimensions of the mental life, indigenous psychology plays an important role in the development of a global psychology" (p. 6). It is not quite clear what this means, but this formulation could be an argument that IPs should unite with postmodern and postcolonial research traditions. If so, it may have the effect of leaving the practical applied aspects of IPs behind.

The question of whether there is one IP approach, or many, also relates to their nature and is reflected in the IP literature. Most IP authors seem to agree that the multiplicity of the various IPs should be recognized (e.g., Nikora, 2007; Sundararajan et al., 2013). However, some researchers have argued as if there is only one IP: see, for example, Kim, Yang, and Hwang (2006b) and Shams (2005). This may be risky, since one of the driving forces behind the IP movement is the desire to avoid the dominance of external actors (traditionally from the West). As can be seen from the earlier quote by Sundararajan et al. (2017, p. 2), these authors also showed a clear tendency to describe the variety of IPs as basically one entity, and Yang (2012), similarly, at an abstract level, discussed IPs as one discipline with a methodology. However, Yang simultaneously recognized that IPs exist in many versions.

A further aspect of the nature of Ips relates to the question of what the general aim of IP research should be. This issue has both political and moral aspects. As we have seen, more or less all IP authors would presumably agree that Ips should aim to improve the applicability of psychological research in non-Western countries by making it more fitted to the local society, including improving the well-being of minorities that have been poorly treated by the larger society. In addition to this, other aims have been suggested, such as enriching psychology by making it more globally representative. This aim is presumably also uncontroversial. A more controversial aim relates to whether Ips should support nation building in the sense that psychology should put itself in the service of nationalism in a country. Here IP researchers have voiced different opinions. Yang (2012) argued clearly against the idea that IP should be in the service of nationalism: "As a discipline, a Non-Western IZP may have nothing to do with the researcher's nationalistic sentiments. This is especially true of the Chinese IZP as developed in Taiwan, Hong Kong, and China" (p. 21). This assertion may be inspired by the sensitive political situation in the Chinese context.

However, the postcolonial birth context of Ips resonates well with a political nationalistic dimension in IP. In line with this, other IP researchers have argued that IP should support nationalism. For example, as described earlier, Enriquez explicitly advocated that Filipino IP should serve a political function by helping to support a national consciousness, and this IP was intentionally developed in order to promote nationalism (see, e.g., Church and Katigbak, 2002). Similarly, Canadian IP was at least partly developed in order to promote nationalistic interests (compare, e.g., Adair, 1999).

In accordance with this, Liu (2011) proclaimed a specific political function of Ips, namely as a means to protect the build-up of nationalism in the IP researchers' countries. Liu (2011, p. 134) wrote: "Finally, many indigenous psychologies are rooted to societies where nationalism is perceived as an important bulwark against internal chaos, western colonization, and outside threats." Liu also argued, against Allwood (2011a), that this provides a political component to Ips, and that this component is more important than taking a theoretical interest in how culture is conceptualized. The latter he saw as potentially internally divisive for Ips. This illustrates the political aspect of Ips, and it also shows the stake-holder dimension of culture – that is, issues relating to who (e.g., what category of people) will have a say in how the culture of a country is constructed. For example, it is not always self-evident for minority groups in a country that the current national agenda serves their interest as the story accounting for their culture.

4.2 Definition of Culture

IP researchers differ in their definitions of culture. A challenge for IPs is to coordinate what they mean by culture with the goals for their IP. Definitions of culture can vary with respect to how broad and inclusive they are: do they focus foremost on the meaning content of people in a culture, or do they also include people's behavior and man-made objects (cultural artifacts)? I will mostly discuss how various IP researchers have conceptualized cultural meaning contents, although the other components of culture can also be argued to be important.

Focusing on meaning contents, definitions of culture range from treating culture as quite abstract, essentialist, and unchanging, to viewing culture as more interactive and dynamically changing. Among the more abstract and essentialist definitions of culture is the one by Berry and Triandis (2006, p. 50): "First, culture emerges in adaptive interactions between humans and environments. Second, culture consists of shared elements. Third, culture is transmitted across time periods and generations." Similar to this, but possibly still more essentialist, is the culture concept promoted in different texts by Hwang. In Hwang's view, the central part of culture consists of "cultural heritage" (that is, very slowly changing tradition). In line with this, Hwang (2006) argued that cultures have deep structures and he (2011a, p. 128) asserted that "[a]s people of a given culture contemplate the nature of the universe and the situation of mankind, they gradually formulate their worldviews with original thinking over the course of their history." Hwang also argued that although people may be unaware of these deep structures, they can be made explicit by researchers taking a structural perspective, and he (2006) concluded that it is an important goal of IPs in East Asia to identify the deep structures of cultural traditions. More recently, Dudgeon et al. (2017) expressed a somewhat similar collectivistic view: "culture may be thought of as a body of collectively shared values, principles, practices, customs, and traditions" (p. 320).

Other IP researchers have provided definitions of culture that show signs of both essentialism and interactionism. Kim has tended to hold on to a more traditional, abstract, and collectivistic view of culture, but also seems to allow for some effects on culture of interactions in a society (e.g., Kim & Park, 2005, 2006). For example, Kim and Park (2006) presented a concept of culture which showed distinct essentialist features, but they also allowed for variation within such a culture. Some parts of their culture concept are in line with that of Kim and Berry (1993a). For instance, they wrote that "[c]ulture represents *the collective utilization of natural and human resources to achieve desired outcomes* (Kim 2001). Culture is defined as *a rubric of patterned variables*" (p. 34, italics in original). They also approvingly cited Shweder's idea that we relate to the world through culture, and argued that "in order to understand a culture, we need to understand its history, and the present and future aspirations of its people" (p. 36).

These quotes give a clear impression of culture as an independent essentialized entity, but, as noted earlier, Kim and Park (2006) allowed for change in that they argued that a culture can be given new interpretations and be changed by new generations. They also noted that there are different philosophies, religions, and worldviews that are in competition, and that "researchers should not automatically assume that Chinese will follow the Confucian way or that Hindu Dharma will automatically explain the behavior of Indians" (p. 40; for similar statements, see Kim & Park, 1999; Sundararajan et al., 2017). These quotes signal that the authors allow for functional effects of the diversity of understandings within a culture, thereby weakening the assumed usefulness of "mono-focused" descriptions of cultures. It is interesting to note that Kim and Park (2006) also argued that the Confucian concepts children learn in school are not the concepts they use in ordinary life and, because of this, researchers have to translate such concepts into psychological constructs.

Such a position is somewhat similar to that of Yang (2012), who appeared to hold an essentialist idea of culture, such as when he wrote: "non-Western cultures have been contaminated by Euro-American culture through the process of Western-dominated modernization" (p. 13). Likewise, when he discussed Western psychology (labelled IP in Yang's terminology), he wrote: "The IP knowledge system has the Euro-American native culture as its indigenous root and is produced through Western theories, concepts, methods, and tools as if it were universally or cross-culturally applicable" (p. 14). Here, Yang seems to neglect the steady influence on Western culture by cultures in other places such as India and the Middle East. In general, it would seem reasonable to argue that cultures are never pure, but always *mixed*.

In other ways, Yang (2012) appears to assume a priori that cultures have a fair degree of homogeneity. Thus, for example, he suggested that researchers should use their own empathetic ability and their tacit knowledge about their culture to try to imagine what a potential participant might think or do in a specific situation. In this context, Yang (2012) suggested that the researcher is psychologically and behaviorally similar to other society members, including the research participants. This, he observed, can help the researcher to understand the participants and promote indigenous compatibility of the research. However, the concept of "society" used here is not quite clear. For example, it is reasonable to ask whether Yang in the cited statement includes research on Taiwanese ethnic minorities (approximately 2% of the population), or only people from the largest ethnic group in Taiwan (Taiwanese, approximately 70%), or something else. Furthermore, Yang may not sufficiently attend to the fact that in most Non-Western countries researchers tend to be quite Westernized and to live in conditions that differ from those of large sections of the remaining population. This might make it more difficult to carry out such exercises in empathetic ability mentioned by Yang (for research showing some of what might be required, see e.g., Banerjee & Duflo, 2011; Gadamer, 1960/ 1985; Mullainathan & Shafir, 2013).

Despite this, Yang's (2012) position shows some consistency, since he also recognizes that people can indeed activate meaning contents from different cultures at different points in time. For example, he observed that when researchers in Non-Western societies do research they "temporarily become Westerners in the sense that they think and act like a Western psychologist in their research activities with respect to conceptualizing, theorizing, designing, data-collecting, and results-interpreting. They no longer experience themselves as a carrier of local culture, but instead as a carrier of Western culture" (p. 22). Here, Yang shows a more interactive and dynamic view of culture.

In recent years, some IP texts appear to promote a more dynamic and interactive culture concept. For example, Sundararajan et al. (2017), on a general level – somewhat enigmatically, and possibly over-totalizing the effect of culture – stated that "[c]ulture constitutes the very fiber of our being – all that we sense, feel, believe, value, think and do" (p. 5). Of interest is that the same authors later in the text (2017, p. 6) stressed the importance of "cultural hybridity" and noted that it has become more common with increasing globalization. Similarly, Sundararajan et al. (2013, p. 70) stated that "even before the era of globalization no culture exists in its pure form." Paradoxically, here the authors also give the impression of retaining essentialism with respect to culture – that is, they seem to assume that there is some definite pure form that cultures might exist in. They (2013) also recognized the hybridity of cultures when they argued for the non-unity of IPs by noting that each culture contains many traditions. However, the same paper (Sundararajan et al. 2013) also described abstract entities such as the indigenous Indian view. By using such descriptions, the authors showed remnants of an approach to culture as a collective, abstract phenomenon. Other IP authors who have suggested culture concepts similar to the more dynamic concept discussed here are Misra, Jain, and Singh (2002), who argued that all interactions between people affect a society's culture to some extent (see also de Souza, 2014).

In general, the newer conceptualizations of culture I have described are in line with recent developments in psychology (and with views in much of social science, including social anthropology). Thus, for example, Weber and Morris (2010) concluded that the external social environment people are in can cause them to *activate* cultural content repertoires from different cultures stored in their memory. Another relevant development in this context is the argument by Morris, Chiu, and Liu (2015) against *culturalism* – that is, the idea that "individuals are shaped by one primary culture and the world's cultural traditions are separate and independent" (p. 633). Instead, they argued for what they called *polyculturalism*: "[that] cultural influence on individuals is partial and plural and cultural traditions interact and change each other" (p. 634). This bears strong similarity to the concept of hybridity. In a description of the larger context of psychologists' understanding of culture, Danziger (2006) observed the irony in that just when psychology has started to realize the importance of culture and cultural differences, cultures are becoming more mixed and cultural differences are starting to disappear.

I have earlier (e.g., Allwood, 2011a) suggested that a more interactive and dynamic culture concept may be of use for IPs that aspire to produce research that is useful in helping to solve local social problems in IP countries. A version of such a culture concept will now be more fully described. This culture concept focuses on the distribution of meaning contents in a society – that is, it heeds that meaning contents in a society are shared to different extents by different groups and individuals, and it recognizes all meaning contents in a society as part of the culture. Thus, from an applied perspective it is relevant to know about the held meaning contents in the part of a society where, for example, a social reform or social-help program is to be implemented. Attention to locally held meaning would include heeding the proportion of males and females involved, and the age and social class of the persons addressed. In general, IPs have not much attended specifically to different categories of people's perception of the world. Understanding in cultures is often treated as one-of-a-kind in IP texts.

Such an interactive and dynamic culture concept also recognizes that meaning is causally generated and is affected through various cognitive and social processes (e.g., Allwood, 2011a; Atran, Medin & Ross, 2005; de Souza, 2014; Kashima, 2005; Shweder, 1990). Assuming that meaning spreads by means of causal social processes (i.e., communication) allows research on, and understanding about, how meaning is generated and spreads in the part of the society where the applied researcher or social helper wants to intervene.

As noted earlier, it is useful to see the culture of a group as including all its current understanding – that is, culture is not just made up of meaning contents reproduced from earlier generations in a society. Culture changes through communication and thinking in specific societies and through global exchanges. Tradition is only a subpart of a culture, and culture is not necessarily very stable. Moreover, in this type of culture concept, meaning is seen as generated on a social arena with actors (stakeholders) promoting their, and their various groups', interests. Furthermore, an important part of the creation of culture is the generation of contents relating to the description of the culture of one's own society. This aspect was well captured by Eagleton (2000), who stressed the political aspects of debates and claims about culture by observing that "[t]he word 'culture', which is supposed to designate a kind of society, is in fact a normative way of imagining that society" (p. 25).

Given this observation, it seems that many IPs may have relied on a conception of their own culture that, at least partly, has been constructed by nationalistic interests. This could have contributed to the reality that IPs in many countries – for example, the Philippines, Taiwan, India, and many African countries – may not have covered the traditions of minority peoples in their countries to a greater extent. However, this danger does not seem to be at hand to the same extent for IPs in, for example, Australia and New Zealand.

A further important aspect of culture, relating to the construction of culture and the issues just discussed, is that ordinary people and politicians often see "their" culture as an important component of their *identity*. Accordingly, different concepts of culture can serve different purposes in IPs. For example, the conventional abstract, collectivistic view of culture held by, for example, Berry and Triandis (2006), may be useful when the aim is to help improve feelings of self-esteem and self-respect in a group of people by promoting, and making more explicit, their conception of their self-identity, as in the type of IP promoted by Nikora (2007) and Dudgeon et al. (2017).

Generally speaking, given that culture is assumed to influence people's thinking and feeling, it is reasonable to pay attention to results from different parts of psychology about how such influence may occur. This is often not attended to in IPs. For example, research results on social psychological processes, such as social learning, model learning, belief in authorities, and conformation tendencies, is helpful for understanding more about the stability and change of cultures and about how meaning contents function in people's everyday life. The same is the case for cognitive psychological research on automatization of cognitive skills, including categorization of events in physical and social reality.

4.3 The Issue of Scientific Standards

An important feature of IPs is that they tend to define themselves as scientific. However, as illustrated above, some IPs seem to deviate from this. This issue was noted by Jahoda (2016), who noted that "in the IP literature there are divergent notions of what is meant by 'scientific', and not all writers believe that IPs need to be scientific" (p. 172).

An aspect of this issue relates to the role of religion in IPs. From early on, IP authors have criticized Western mainstream psychology for its handling of religion. For example, D. Sinha and M. Sinha (1997) noted that in Eastern thought "religion and, philosophy and psychology do not stand sundered," whereas "psychology has remained in sharp contrast to religion in the West" (p. 27). Furthermore, religion is often taken for granted in many non-Western societies (Norenzayan, 2013; Ojalehto & Medin, 2015), and many IPs have an ambition to draw on religious traditions, some of them heavily. This does not necessarily have to create a problem for IPs as long as they simply describe traditional concepts and ideas and how they influence behavior. However, D. Sinha (1997) warned that there is a risk that indigenization may lead to dysfunctional "cultural chauvinism" and "anti-scientific tendencies." For example, some authors "extract from ancient sources speculative views about phenomena whose only claim to validity is their ancient origin" (Sinha, p. 158). Similarly, Sundararajan et al. (2017) warned that IP authors too often use philosophical and religious texts when they attempt to explain psychological phenomena. Kim et al. (1999) and Kim and Park (2006) issued similar warnings.

Some versions of IP – for example Indian, Iranian, and Pakistani IPs – provide clear cases where the distinction between science and religion is not always apparent. Moreover, the issue about what should count as scientific standards has been raised by Enriquez in the context of writing about whether the conception of scientific research should be seen as an international, or Eastern, accomplishment. Thus, he wrote (1997, p. 43), "[a]s research on indigenous psychology matured, it became clear that the West did not enjoy the monopoly on scientific standards. In fact, the recognition that science evolved from Eastern intellectual traditions provided additional impetus to the task of investigating the Filipino intellectual tradition."

The question of scientific standards really comes to the fore in the context of so-called *Islamic psychology*. In his description of the two camps in Islamic psychology, Long (2014, p. 18) argued that none of these camps has produced a credibly Islamicized psychology. Irrespective of whether the attempt to Islamicize the discipline is from within or from without, the issue of secularization has not been resolved. It is easy to agree, because a central feature of science is that it ultimately is sensitive to empirical evidence; that is, no prior postulates, such as those in a religious text, can be given a priori precedence. Science is defined by a belief that human understanding is ultimately sensitive to empirical evidence. Accordingly, if the boundary between science and religion is softened it is likely to be more difficult to evaluate empirical evidence in an unbiased way.

Such IPs, and statements such as Enriquez's (1997, p. 43), would be targets for Jahoda's concern about the definition of "scientific." Jahoda (2016) also worried about the fact that many IP authors "suggest that their IPs should in the main be based on their own traditions. Mention is made of Buddhist, Confucian and Hindu religions and philosophies, all of which contain significant psychological elements" (p. 175). An example of Jahoda's worry might be Yang's (2012) assertion that "local researchers should try to be a typical native in the cultural sense as they design and conduct a study, and ... they should let their indigenous ideas, tacit knowledge (in Polanyi's sense), and native ways of thinking be fully reflected in the whole research process" (p. 22) The reader may ask, if the researcher is to think from the basis of the local culture as it appears to be envisioned by Yang, how does this match with the ambition to conduct research according to scientific standards? This problem does not only concern groups lacking Western-style education, since much research has shown that people educated in modern Western societies also often fail to follow scientific standards in their thinking (see, e.g., Nisbett & Ross, 1980). Thus, the issue is not necessarily to identify which culture scientific standards are to be based on, but rather to identify the scientific standards as such. The need for postgraduate training in any country suggests that scientific standards belong to a very specialized branch of understanding based on preunderstanding that does not exclusively belong to any specific culture.

In brief, should IPs be seen as "scientific?" Jahoda (2016) noted the problem that many IPs wanted to have the prestige associated with science, yet did not want to be confined by the strictures of research methodology. This dilemma, Jahoda argued, has often resulted in science being redefined in more flexible ways. Similarly, Ho (1998) concluded that not all IPs are scientific, because some of them do not follow "the principles and methods [of] time-honored canons of science (e.g., capability of being falsified)" (p. 94).

The influence of postmodernist authors, such as Kenneth Gergen, on IPs might contribute to the view that IP researchers will increasingly choose not to adhere to more conventional definitions of science. If so, this could lead to decreased pragmatic utility and possibly also isolation from the international research community. It is obvious that the question of whether IPs are scientific cannot be answered in simple terms because, as has been amply illustrated, the various IPs differ in their methodological approach. However, it seems clear that some IPs, as described by, for example, Furlow (1996) and Long (2014), would not be classified as scientific. Thus, a reasonable conclusion, similar to Ho's (1998), seems to be that some – probably most – IPs are scientific and some – probably a minority – are not.

4.4 Views on the Philosophy of Science and of Mainstream Psychology

A further challenge for IPs is to provide a convincing description of their approach at a theoretical meta-level – that is, in terms of concepts used in the philosophy of science. As illustrated below, different writers in IP occasionally show a somewhat unreflected understanding of the philosophy of science.

An example of such understanding involves IP authors who, often uncritically, appear to assume a distinction between natural sciences and human sciences (henceforth: the N/H-distinction). Such a distinction tended to be popular in the social sciences in the 1970s, but developments in research in the last half-century have meant that the N/H-distinction is not taken as self-evident anymore, or is simply not accepted. In fact, taking this distinction to depict a qualitative difference between two types of science is often seen as problematic and controversial (see e.g., Allwood, 2012). This integrative development in research has been strengthened by recent developments in cognitive science (including artificial intelligence) and the life sciences, where researchers have provided evidence of close connections between naturalistic and humanistic phenomena – for example, between brain and mind.

It is somewhat surprising that IPs, which tend to be based on the IP researchers' own cultures, find it relevant to position themselves in relation to the Western-derived N/H-distinction. Moreover, it is not clear how arguing for a separation between naturalistic and humanistic research relates to the IP researchers' culture. For example, it is frequently pointed out that human beings and nature are commonly seen as more integrated in Indian and East Asian religions than in Western thinking (see, e.g., Chapple, 2002; Nisbett, 2003; Randerson, 2015). However, the N/H-distinction often appears to be accepted in the IP literature, where it has one of its remaining strongholds. An early example is Kim and Berry (1993a), who seemed to identify IPs with the cultural sciences: "the indigenous psychologies approach represented in this volume is a direct descendant of Wundt's Geisteswissenschaften tradition"

(p. 1); they also claimed that the "lineage" of IPs can be linked to the tradition of what they called "cultural science". Other IP authors (e.g., Hwang, 2013a; Sinha, 2002; Yang, 2012) have concurred.

As illustrated next, some IP authors appear to hold a somewhat limited understanding of modern psychology and this may facilitate upholding the N/H-distinction. For example, Kim, Park, and Park (1999) used a concept they called "traditional psychology" to mean Western psychology up to about the 1970s, but which more obviously represents behaviorism in the first part of the twentieth century. Thus, their concept of "traditional psychology" is unclear, and is then used as a straw man to create a contrast to their Korean IP. Moreover, Kim and Park (2006) argued that in general psychology "the mind is considered a black box" (p. 29). Along the same lines, Kim and Park (2005) also wrote that "[g]eneral psychology has adopted positivism in search of abstract and universal laws of human behavior and eliminated the subjective aspects of human functioning (i.e. agency, meaning, intention and goals) and the influence of context and culture" (p. 75). It is not likely that many researchers involved in research in mainstream psychology in the twenty-first century would recognize this description as accurate!

Similarly, Sundararajan et al. (2017) upheld the N/H-distinction by means of a controversial understanding of psychology when they argued that "[g]eneral psychology represents the natural sciences approach, and indigenous psychology represents the cultural science tradition" (p. 1). However, many – maybe most – researchers in psychology may not agree that general psychology represents the natural sciences approach, partly because the N/H-distinction, as it is conventionally used, appears too coarse and as outdated. In addition, it is not clear what should currently be meant by the "natural science approach," as illustrated by the historical perspective taken in evolutionary astrophysics.

Sundararajan et al. (2017) also provided other controversial and seemingly outdated renderings of research in psychology. For example, they claimed that, in contrast to physics and the biological sciences, in the human sciences the researcher needs to know people's intentions, and their goals and motives. Moreover, they argued that such information can be found by studying people's self-reports. However, researchers in psychology are likely to disagree, for various reasons. For example, it is not clear why this information would not be relevant also in biology. Moreover, with respect to self-reports, Nisbett and Wilson (1977), in their well-known paper *Telling More Than We Can Know: Verbal Reports on Mental Processes*, showed that humans are not always trustworthy reporters of the sources of their behavior.

A further example of controversial assumptions made in IPs that relate to the philosophy of science is in Hwang's (2011b) criticism of a number of methodological approaches to comparisons of results from different societies suggested by IP researchers. The reason for his criticism was that such approaches assume an inductive approach, in contrast to Popper's anti-inductive, deductive falsification approach. These approaches included Enriquez's *cross-indigenous method* (to compare results from IPs working with emic from-within approaches in order to look for higher-order generalizations) and *the derived etic approach* (to compare the results from etic and emic approaches) suggested by Berry and Kim (1993). In a debate between myself (e.g., Allwood, 2013b) and Hwang on this issue, Hwang (2013b) expressed his admiration for Popper's philosophy. However, arguments showing the limitations of Popper's falsificationism have been available for a long time in the philosophy of science literature, and it is not clear that falsificationism is very much safer than inductionism. In a brilliant paper, Earp and Trafimow (2015) showed convincingly why Popper's falsification is not a more reasonable or stable path to follow in research than verification (or, as expressed by Hwang, inductionism). For example, results that appear to falsify a theory might as well be due to the falsifying study being a poor study in any of a number of ways.

Yet a further example of controversial standpoints relating to the philosophy of science is that some IP researchers appear to equate positivism and analysis of causality (e.g., Sinha, 2002). However, one can clearly carry out studies analyzing causal relations without being a positivist (e.g., Shadish, Cook & Campbell, 2002). Moreover, authors such as Maxwell (2004a,b) argue that causal analysis is compatible with qualitative research. Similarly, there is no necessary contradiction between understanding meaning content and explaining it since it is reasonable to argue, as many authors have done, that meaning and understanding are naturalistic phenomena that are causally linked to the rest of nature (e.g., Allwood, 2011a; Atran et al., 2005; de Souza, 2014; Kashima, 2005; Shweder, 1990).

4.5 Generalizations

IP researchers have criticized Western psychology historically, and maybe even for continuing to do so today, for overgeneralizing results (often based on students) from the West to the rest of the world. However, published statements by IP researchers sometimes also contain overgeneralizations – or at least it is unclear if it is possible to generalize to the intended population. It is noteworthy that this tendency to overgeneralize has previously been warned against in the

IP literature. Abdi (1975) noted that although all Africans are from Africa and hence tend to be from developing countries, Africans from a particular country tend to differ from Africans from another country, and therefore one should not generalize findings from one part of Africa to the whole continent: "In order to understand Africans one must be familiar with the foundation of their cultures, history and socio-economic situations" (p. 231).

Enriquez's conclusions about Filipino personality as representative of people living in the Philippines, and assertions by Sundararajan et al. (2013, p. 18) about "the indigenous Indian view," illustrate potential overgeneralizations, or at least cases with unclear bases for generalizing. That it is unreasonable to speak about *the* indigenous Indian view in the singular becomes abundantly clear in Wendy Doniger's (2009) beautiful book *The Hindus: An alternative history*. Parenthetically, there is even a debate on whether Hinduism should be seen as one or many religions (see, e.g., Llewellyn, 2005). A further example of potential overgeneralization is Oppong's (2016) discussion of *the African personality*, despite the empirical grounds for making statements about this very abstract entity appearing shaky. Similarly, Hwang (2013a) recommended that IPs do research on "the particular mentality of people within a given society" (p. 717).

The suggestion to study what is common to more or less all Africans, and similar suggestions in other IPs, resembles the work on national character that has been ongoing at least since the nineteenth century. For example, psychological anthropological studies in the culture and personality school often assumed a typical personality for a society. However, current systematic research has found little support for the reality of national characters (e.g. Shiraev & Levy, 2013; Terracciano et al., 2005). McCrae and Terracciano (2006) concluded that research exploring the assessment of personality profiles in more than fifty "cultures" shows that perceived national characters are unfounded, and such perceptions were described as stereotypes. Similarly Shiraev and Levy (2013, p. 918) concluded that studies in this area "do not provide clear evidence that people of particular nations have strong personality features different from people in other nations."

Another illustration of possibly oversimplified generalizations, this time pertaining also to cross-cultural psychologists, is Poortinga's (2016) criticism of IP authors for being too simplistic in the use of the distinction between collectivistic and individualistic societies. In this context, Poortinga cited a study by D. Sinha and Tripathi (1994) that found indications of both individualism and collectivism in India. It is also relevant that Cross and Madson (1997) found women in the USA to be just as collectivistic as many groups in Asia. Despite this, many IP authors characterize, for example, the whole (or large chunks) of Asia or Africa as collectivistic and the West as individualistic. For instance, Ho (1998, p. 91) argued that "[c]onstructs like actor, ego, self, and personality reflect an individualistic conception of human existence character-istic of the West. In contrast, constructs such as face, relational orientation, and relational identity reflect a relational conception characteristic of Confucian culture." However, although not all Chinese are Confucians and some non-Chinese are, it is noteworthy that research relating broadly to Chinese people has often been found not to generalize within this category of people (Smith, 2010).

It is also noteworthy that, in general, current Western mainstream psychol-ogy is slowly taking a more interactive and complex perspective to research issues, especially in applied research but also in basic research. Taking such an interactive perspective is presumably a more realistic stand, not least because social reality as such has always been interactive within and between societies, and may recently have become even more interactive, partly due to the Internet.

4.6 The Issues of Isolation and Independence

IP researchers have discussed whether IPs should utilize, and thereby possi-bly be influenced by, the work of researchers in other countries, or whether it is best for IPs to only use their own cultural and language resources. In general, isolation can be seen as breaking one of the norms for science suggested by the sociologist of science Robert Merton. This is the norm about *universalism* – that is, that all researchers should have an equal chance to be heard and to influence research (see, e.g., Ziman, 2000). Different IP authors have answered this question differently, sometimes even authors from the same country.

Some IP authors have argued for isolation. The clearest example may be Enriquez in the Philippines and the *Sikolohiyang Pilipino* (SP), although he (1977) also wrote about the cross-indigenous method as a strategy to make psychology more truly global: "The cross-indigenous method is a call for the multi-language–multi-culture approach based on indigenous viewpoints" (p. 16). However, in general, SP has sometimes celebrated the benefits of cultural and language isolation – i.e., not to partake of research literature written in other countries (especially not researchers from the West) and not to write, for example, research papers, in English or other non-Filipino languages. More specifically, the desire to develop an authentic IP seems to be associated with the idea that there is such a thing as complete cultural purity and that such a state means not being influenced by any concepts or ideas other than those existing in one's near cultural environment. The popularity of such ideas has decreased substantially since the nineteenth century, and these types of reasons for isolation seem outdated. A further reason for isolation may be a fear of being overrun by ideas, mainly from the West, and specifically the USA. However, isolation may be a poor strategy to reach a high-quality level in one's research output.

A further example of isolation in IPs is Canadian IP, criticized by Kim and Park (2005), as discussed earlier, for not being a "real" IP. There were likely multiple driving forces for the development of IP in Canada, one of which seems to have been the feeling that the Canadian reality was not well represented in the US psychology textbooks commonly in use in Canada. Another was a feeling that too many US psychologists were taking academic positions in Canada and that Canadians were thus being accorded a secondary position in their own country. Instead, as described by Adair (1999), hiring committees were instructed to employ Canadian academics first. Again, this appears to be a clear break with Merton's norm relating to universalism, caused partly by a desire for psychological research to be more representative of the Canadian reality, and partly by academic self-interest.

Manfusa Shams (2002) has also argued for the necessity to keep IPs free from external influences. Her reason was the "dominant position of western indigenous psychologies" (p. 88). Interestingly enough, she suggested that the way to accomplish this purity is through "frequent exchange of theoretical dialogue and empirical research collaboration between non-western and western indigenous psychologies" (p. 89).

Yang (e.g., 2012) also discussed isolation. His approach may, at least initially, seem to be one of moderation compared to that of Enriquez. An example is Yang's assertion that non-Western IP researchers should pay attention to Western researchers' experiences and methods because these may be useful when creating theories and methods in IPs. But he attempted to strike a balance by arguing that IP researchers should never, from sheer habit and uncritically, begin their research from the starting-point of theories, methods, and other products of Western research. Instead, they should first identify a local interesting phenomenon and then thoroughly learn to understand the concrete local features of the studied context, including the experiences and behavior of the local people.

Other statements by Yang (2012) show more clear isolation tendencies. For example, he argued that in order to produce research with high indigenous compatibility, IP researchers trained in the West should use their native language when carrying out research. In this way they can avoid filtering out specific aspects that belong to the indigenous context. Yang ends by espousing a quite radical stance on the isolation issue: "In order to obtain the truly indigenized accomplishments with high IC needed for the development of IZP, non-Western psychologists must refrain from thinking and behaving as Western psychologists and try to be a typical native when functioning as researchers" (p. 22). Adding complexity to his position, Yang (2012), also argued that complete indigenization is not possible.

Many authors in IPs have argued *against* isolation, using different kinds of arguments. Some have criticized IPs for taking an isolationist stand; a clear representative of this group is D. Sinha (1997), who warned against "parochialism in knowledge, built on a kind of Western vs non-Western dichotomy" (p. 159). Sinha saw such parochialism as ill-conceived, and he argued that knowledge should not be "circumscribed by national and regional borders" (p. 159). Finally, he also stated that "indigenization by its very definition does not imply cultural duality of knowledge, but essentially endeavors to bring about an interface of the two to their mutual advantage" (p. 159).

Ho (1998) also argued that IP should be open and interactive, and that it should not try to avoid influence from other parts of the world. Avoiding such influence might lead to IP becoming conservative and self-sufficient. He also warned that such isolation might "degenerate into an indiscriminate rejection of Western psychology" (p. 89). In contrast, he argued that including foreign concepts may lead to a healthy synthesis of ideas from different places. Adair (1992) went further and argued that "[m]ost would agree that an indigenous psychology should resemble the North American discipline, although its variables and theories will reflect the local culture" (p. 62). This assertion is presumably quite controversial in the IP context. Adair (1996) also warned that use of "native language labels" could lead to unfruitful arguments about definitions and distance IPs from international developments. In the same vein, Kim and Park (2006) criticized work on researching indigenous concepts as being of limited value to researchers who do not know the language or know the researched phenomenon firsthand. Moreover, they argued that it is difficult to know if the results from this type of research are correct, or even to know their scientific value since not much research supports the conclusions from this research.

As noted earlier, Hwang (e.g., 2005, 2015) exemplifies an IP author who has wholeheartedly argued that IP researchers should not limit themselves to influences only from their own culture. Hwang argued that it is necessary for IPs to use Western philosophies of science in order to promote and make progress in their research. For example, he wrote: "It is one of my eternal beliefs that in order to overcome the difficulties encountered in the work of theoretical construction, non-Western IPists have to understand not only their own cultural tradition, but also the Western philosophy of science" (2015, pp. 9–10). From this he argued that IP researchers should use the philosophical frameworks he prefers, namely those of the philosopher and sociologist Roy Bhaskar and his critical realism, and the philosopher Fritz Wallner and con- structive realism. Doing this would make IP researchers able to compete with researchers in Western mainstream psychology. Similarly, de Souza (2014) suggested that IPs should adopt a Western-derived framework, namely critical realism.

Given the various arguments presented above, it would seem that IPs may be better served by not isolating themselves and thereby limiting themselves to information and meaning from their own culture. One reason for this conclusion is that creativity studies and research in science studies have tended to support the good effects on creativity and innovation of sharing understanding deriving from a broad range of backgrounds. Thus, such research has in general supported the usefulness of openness as an approach to research (see, e.g., Hemlin, Allwood & Martin, 2008; Hemlin et al., 2013a,b). Finally, IPs hopefully will also, as most of them currently do, keep adhering to conventional scientific standards as they develop over time, irrespective of the extent to which these currently or historically have been influenced by Western thinking.

5 Conclusions

One important reason for the development of the IP movement was discontent with the lack of fit of Western psychology with the local realities in non- Western or non-US societies. It is interesting to consider why Western psychology may have a poor predictive ability. One reason is illustrated by the so-called WEIRD study (Henrich et al., 2010). This study found that major classical findings in Western psychology did not replicate well in other cultural contexts. One cause for this, as argued by the authors, is that US students show differences from US citizens in general, and that these differ from other Westerners, and that Westerners differ from other people on the globe.

Moreover, although geographical proximity may be a general indicator for cultural closeness as postulated by diffusionism, it is not always a safe indicator of similarity in understanding and behavior. This is shown, for example, in research by Atran et al. (2005) on the attitude to, and use of, nature by three different Indian groups in Guatemala (Itza, Landinos, and high- and lowland Quetcha). Moreover, in today's world, with ever-increasing international exchange, the simple division between West and non-West may increasingly prove to be too simplistic, as may, for example, the division between collectivistic and individualistic societies, as discussed earlier (e.g., Poortinga, 2016). Whether the society is urban or rural, modern or traditional, may be of equal importance. In addition, many issues may be common to minority groups – for example, their relation to the majority population.

However, apart from these and other differences, a further reason why results from Western psychology may replicate poorly in non-Western contexts is that, as found in multiple studies, psychological research replicates poorly also in Western contexts, sometimes even more so than research in the other social sciences. For example, the Open Science Collaboration (2015) study found that only one-third of the studies in top-notch psychological journals could be replicated in new studies which attempted to closely reflect the conditions in the first studies.

This volume has illustrated the great heterogeneity of IPs. As formulated by Pe-Pua (2015, p. 790) "the development of IP in various countries [shows that] there is no single path for developing IP. Each country has their particularities in terms of national history, policies, priorities, and positioning in the academic environment." An important feature of IPs' research programs is that they should be based on the culture of the IP researcher's society, and this ambition, by itself, may have had the effect of creating heterogeneity among IPs. A further contributing reason for the diversity of IPs is that they have attempted to reach different types of goals. The heterogeneity of IPs may also have been influenced by the contributions of a limited number of active individual researchers in each country, such as Virgio Enriquez, Durganand Sinha, Kuo-Shu Yang, Bame Nsamenang, Linda Waimarie Nikora, and Pat Dudgeon, each with their own specific inclinations. The importance of such strong men and women should be further evaluated in future research.

In addition, IPs, for example in India and Iran, show interesting internal variation. Some of the larger IPs include research that is fairly close to main-stream psychological research, research on traditional concepts, and research inspired by critical approaches such as postmodernism, postcolonialism, and feminism. Further studies on IPs would profit by more detailed exploration of the factors that cause such heterogeneity in IPs within a country.

The preparation of the present work has shown that obtaining a clear under-standing of the current state of IPs in different countries is problematic. More detailed studies of indigenization processes in different countries and of the current state of their IPs would be desirable. Such studies should preferably include not simply qualitative judgments from more or less involved research-ers, but clear appropriate quantitative information. Adair and Gabrenya and their colleagues have been pioneers in this type of research on IPs. Examples of such quantitative information are the proportion of IP articles (of all published psychological articles from the nation researched), or the number and proportion of conferences, or sessions in conferences, relating to IPs. At the same time, such studies would need clear definitions with respect, for example, to criteria for deciding when an article should be classified as coming from an IP.

In general, IPs have moved the focus of research from abstract high-level comparisons between countries (typical for cross-cultural psychology) to somewhat more local and detailed studies of psychological issues in specific nations. Despite this, many IP researchers, in line with tendencies in cross-cultural psychology, have carried out studies on abstract entities such as the Filipino consciousness, Confucian concepts, or concepts from Hinduism, and often described their results as relating to the national level, or similar abstract units. Such IP research has, in contrast to the IPs in, for example, Australia and New Zealand, more rarely been conducted at the level of specific ethnic groups. In general, results relating to high levels of aggregation, such as large nations or cultures, may not necessarily generalize well within that unit. Many of the examples provided by Doniger (2009) of the specific versions of Hindu concepts and myths in local ethnic groups or in other social categories show the potential fruitfulness of studying conceptualizations in local contexts.

Finally, the future of IP is interesting to consider. Jahoda (2016), in his critical paper about IPs, suggested that it is an approach in decline. Even the more developed IPs, such as that in the Philippines, do not seem to have grown larger than being simply one of many alternative courses in psychology in their own country (Church & Katigbak, 2002). However, some researchers, for example Sundararajan et al. (2017), seem quite sanguine about the future of IP and have predicted a larger influence of postmodernism and postcolonial approaches.

Apart from IP, there is a general trend toward internationalization in psychology. For example, researchers in many non-Western or non-US countries are in the process of adapting the results of psychology to conditions in their own countries. This is done by, for example, revising scales and questionnaires and by testing the replicability of results from other countries. But this type of work may not commonly be seen as doing indigenous psychology. It is simply general common sense if one is interested in applying previous research carried out in another country in one's own country (Shadish et al., 2002). A further example of internalization is that a great deal of research is carried out relating to the psychology of people in non-Western countries without that research being explicitly labelled as IP. A good example is the vast anthology *Oxford handbook of Chinese psychology*, edited by Michael Harris Bond, where, although it obviously pertains to Chinese psychology, Bond (2010), in his preface, does not refer to IP, and the book's index does not include "indigenous psychology" or even the term "indigenous" (apart from one mention of "Indigenous facial stimulation materials, development of").

Yet a further example of the increasing interest in internationalizing psychology is division 52, *International Psychology*, of the APA and its journal *International Perspectives in Psychology Research, Practice, Consultation*, inaugurated in 2012. It is interesting that Gibbons and Carr (2016), in an editorial for this journal, did not find it relevant to mention IP. The editorial described the journal as "designed to extend psychological knowledge both geographically and thematically" (Gibbons & Carr, 2016, p. 207), and noted that its goals overlap remarkably with the sustainable development goals launched by the United Nations in 2016.

A further issue pertaining to the future of IP relates to the type of IPs developed in Australia and New Zealand. These are aimed at concretely supporting specific minority peoples who have not fared well, at least partly due to maltreatment by the majority society. Such IPs appear to be carrying out very useful practical work and give an impression of enthusiasm and energy. At the same time these types of IPs raise the by now classical question in the IP literature: How many IPs can and should be developed?

This question was raised by D. Sinha (1997) and Poortinga (1999). Sinha (1997) asked if each village should have its own IP. In many countries where IPs could be developed it may be unrealistic to think that this will happen due to a lack of resources for research. However, in general, the national level may often not be the most relevant level for IPs. In order to be more efficient in providing relevant research to their societies, it may often be better for IP researchers to concentrate on conditions and circumstances in smaller-scale community environments, as is done in IP in New Zealand, Australia, Canada, and the USA. Such a localized approach has the potential to concretely help the members of the groups studied and is in line with other developments in international psychology (for this type of approach in the USA, see Stringer, 2018).

In brief, given the increasing diversification of IP, including a tendency to be increasingly linked to other ongoing intellectual waves such as critical theory and postcolonialism, and given the tendency for other forms of globalized and internationalized psychology to develop, the IP movement might in the future dissolve into different versions, more or less aligned and associated with other developments in psychology. At the same time, some of the more applied components in IP research programs may be at least partially covered by other approaches to psychology.

References

Abdi, Y. O. (1975). The problem and prospects of psychology in Africa. *International Journal of Psychology, 10*, 227–234. doi:10.1080/00207597508247334

Adair, J. G. (1992). Empirical studies of indigenization and development of the discipline in developing countries. In S. Iwawaki, Y. Kashima, & K. Leung (Eds.), *Innovations in cross-cultural psychology* (pp. 62–74). Lisse: Swets & Zeitlinger.

Adair, J. G. (1995). The research environment in developing countries: Contributions to the national development of the discipline. *International Journal of Psychology, 30*, 643–662. doi:10.1080/00207599508246592

Adair, J. G. (1996). The indigenous psychology bandwagon: Cautions and considerations. In J. Pandey, D. Sinha, & D. P. S. Bhawuk (Eds.), *Asian contributions to cross-cultural psychology* (pp. 50–58). London: Sage Publications.

Adair, J. G. (1998). Factors facilitating and impeding psychology's contribution to national development. *InterAmerican Journal of Psychology, 32*, 13–32.

Adair, J. G. (1999). Indigenization of psychology: The concept and its practical implementation. *Applied Psychology: An International Review, 48*, 403–418. doi:10.1111/j.1464-0597.1999.tb00062.x

Adair, J. G. (2006). Creating indigenous psychologies: Insights from empirical social studies of the science of psychology. In U. Kim, K.-S. Yang, & K.-K. Hwang (Eds.), *Indigenous and cultural psychology: Understanding people in context* (pp. 467–485). New York: Springer.

Adair, J. G., & Diaz-Loving, R. (1999). Indigenous psychologies: The meaning of the concept and its assessment: Introduction. *Applied Psychology: An International Review, 48*, 397–402. doi:10.1111/j.1464-0597.1999.tb00061.x

Adair, J. G., Kashima, Y., Maluf, M. R., & Pandey, J. (2009). Beyond indigenization: International dissemination of research by majority-world psychologists. In A. Gari & K. Mylonas (Eds.), *Quod Erat Demonstrandum (Q. E. D.): From Heroditus' ethnographic journeys to cross-cultural research* (pp. 59–68). Athens: Pedio Books.

Allwood, C. M. (2011a). On the foundation of the indigenous psychologies. *Social Epistemology, 25*, 3–14. doi:10.1080/02691728.2010.534564

Allwood, C. M. (2011b). On the use of the culture concept in the indigenous psychologies: Reply to Hwang and Liu. *Social Epistemology, 25*, 155–166. doi:10.1080/02691728.2011.552128

Allwood, C. M. (2012). The distinction between qualitative and quantitative research methods is problematic. *Quality & Quantity, 46*, 1417–1429. doi:10.1007/s11135-011-9455-8

Allwood, C. M. (2013a). Anthropology of knowledge. In K. D. Keith (Ed.), *The encyclopedia of cross-cultural psychology, Vol. 1* (pp. 69–72). Chichester: Wiley-Blackwell. doi:10.1002/9781118339893.wbeccp025

Allwood, C. M. (2013b). The role of culture and understanding in research. *Social Epistemology Review and Reply Collective, 2*(5) 1–11. http://wp.me /p1Bfg0-JL

Allwood, C. M., & Berry, J. W. (2006). Origins and development of indigenous psychologies: An international analysis. *International Journal of Psychology, 41*, 243–268. doi:10.1080/00207590544000013

Arnett, J. J. (2008). The neglected 5%: Why American psychology needs to become less American. *American Psychologist, 63*, 602–614. doi:10.1037/ 0003-066X.63.7.602

Asante, K. O. & Oppong, S. (2012). Psychology in Ghana. *Journal of Psychology in Africa, 22*, 473–476. doi:10.1080/14330237.2012.10820557

Atran, S., Medin, D. L., & Ross, N. O. (2005). The cultural mind: Environmental decision making and cultural modeling within and across populations. *Psychological Review, 112*, 744–776. doi:10.1037/0033-295X.112.4.744

Badri, M. B. (1979). *The dilemma of Muslim psychologists*. London: MWH.

Banerjee, A. V., & Duflo, E. (2011). *Poor economics*. London: Penguin.

Barth, F. (2002). An anthropology of knowledge. *Current Anthropology, 43*, 1–18. doi:10.1086/324131

Basalla, G. (1967). The spread of Western science. *Science, 14*, 611–22. doi:10.1126/science.156.3775.611.

Berry, J. W. (1997). Cruising the world: A nomad in academe. In M. H. Bond (Ed.), *Working at the interface of culture: Eighteen lives in social science* (pp. 138–153). London: Routledge.

Berry, J. W., & Kim, U. (1993). The way ahead: From indigenous psychologies to a universal psychology. In U. Kim & J. W. Berry (Eds.), *Indigenous psychologies: Research and experience in cultural context* (pp. 277–280). Newbury Park: Sage.

Berry, J. W., & Triandis, H. C. (2006). *Culture*. In K. Pawlik & G. d'Ydewalle (Eds.), *Psychological concepts: An international historical perspective* (pp. 47–62). Hove: Psychology Press.

Bond, M. H. (2010). Introduction: Reaching this stage in studying the psychology of the Chinese people. In M. H. Bond (Ed.), *Oxford handbook of Chinese psychology* (pp. 1–4). New York: Oxford University Press.

Chapple, C. K. (Ed.). (2002). *Jainism and ecology: Nonviolence in the web of life*. Cambridge, MA: Harvard Divinity School.

Choi, S.-C., Kim, U., & Choi, S.-H. (1993). Indigenous analysis of collective representations: A Korean perspective. In U. Kim & J. W. Berry (Eds.), *Indigenous psychologies: Research and experience in cultural context* (pp. 193–210). Newbury Park: Sage.

Church, A. T., & Katigbak, M. S. (2002). Indigenization of psychology in the Philippines. *International Journal of Psychology, 37*, 129–148. doi:10.1080/00207590143000315

Cole, M. (1996). *Cultural psychology: A once and future discipline*. Cambridge, MA: Harvard University Press.

Cross, S. E., & Madson, L. (1997). Models of the self: Self-construals and gender. *Psychological Bulletin, 122*, 5–37. doi:10.1037/0033-2909.122.1.5

Dalal, A. K. (1990). India: Psychology in Asia and Pacific. In G. Shouksmith & E. A. Shouksmith (Eds.), *Special report on teaching in eleven countries*. Bangkok: UNESCO.

Danziger, K. (2006). Universalism and indigenization in the history of modern psychology. In A. C. Brock (Ed.), *Internationalizing the history of psychology* (pp. 208–225). New York: New York University Press.

de Souza, D. E. (2014). Culture, context and society – The underexplored potential of critical realism as a philosophical framework for theory and practice. *Asian Journal of Social Psychology, 17*, 141–151. doi:10.1111/ajsp.12052

Diaz-Guerrero, R. (1993). Mexican ethnopsychology. In U. Kim & J. W. Berry (Eds.), *Indigenous psychologies: Research and experience in cultural context* (pp. 44–55). Newbury Park: Sage.

Diaz-Loving, R. (2005). Emergence and contributions of a Latin American indigenous social psychology. *International Journal of Psychology, 40*, 213–227. doi:10.1080/00207590444000168

Diaz-Loving, R. (2015). Roglio Diaz-Guerrero: Pioneer of Latin American psychology. In G. J. Rich & U. P. Gielen (Eds.), *Pathfinders in international psychology* (pp. 175–186). Charlotte: Information Age Publishing, Inc.

Doniger, W. (2009). *The Hindus: An alternative history*. London: Penguin Books.

Dudgeon, P. (2017). Editorial Australian indigenous psychology. *Australian Psychologist, 52*, 251–254. doi:10.1111/ap.12298

Dudgeon, P., Bray, A., D'Costa, B., & Walker, R. (2017). Decolonizing psychology: Validating social and emotional wellbeing. *Australian Psychologist, 52*, 316–325. doi:10.1111/ap.12294

Durojaiye, M. O. (1993). Indigenous psychology in Africa: The search for meaning. In U. Kim & J. W. Berry (Eds.), *Indigenous psychologies: Research and
experience in cultural context* (pp. 211–220). Newbury Park: Sage.

Eagleton, T. (2000). *The idea of culture*. Oxford: Blackwell Publishing.

Earp, B. D., & Trafimow, D. (2015). Replication, falsification, and the crisis of
confidence in social psychology. *Frontiers of Psychology*, *6*, 621. doi:10.3389/
fpsyg.2015.00621

Ebadi, S. (2006). *Iran awakening*. London: Rider.

Enriquez, V. G. (1977). Filipino psychology in the third world. *Philippine
Journal of Psychology*, *10*, 3–18.

Enriquez, V. G. (1993). Developing a Filipino Psychology. In U. Kim &
J. W. Berry (Eds.), *Indigenous Psychologies Research and experience in
cultural context* (pp. 152–169). Newbury Park: Sage Publications.

Enriquez, V. G. (1997). Filipino psychology: Concepts and methods.
In H. S. R. Kao & D. Sinha (Eds.), *Asian perspectives on psychology*
(Vol. 19, Cross-cultural research and methodology series; pp. 40–53).
London: Sage Publications.

Furlow, C. A. (1996). The Islamization of knowledge: Philosophy, legitimation
and politics. *Social Epistemology* (Special issue: *Islamic Social
Epistemology)*, 10, 259–271. doi:10.1080/02691729608578818

Gabrenya, Jr., W. K., Kung, M.-C., & Chen, L.-Y. (2006). Understanding
the Taiwan indigenous psychology movement. A sociology of science
approach. *Journal of Cross-Cultural Psychology*, *37*, 597–622. doi:10.1177/
0022022106290480

Gabrenya, Jr., W. K., & Sun, C.-R. (2015). Kuo-Shu Yang: Scholar, leader,
activist. In G. J. Rich & U. P. Gielen (Eds.), *Pathfinders in international
psychology* (pp. 201–212). Charlotte: Information Age Publishing, Inc.

Gadamer, H. G. (1960/1985). *Truth and method*. New York: The Crossroad
Publishing Company.

García-Martínez, A. T., Guerrero-Bote, V. P., & de Moya-Anegón, F. (2012).
World scientific production in psychology. *Universitas Psychologica*, *11*,
699–717.

Gastardo-Conaco, M. C. (2005). The development of a Filipino indigenous
psychology. *Philippine Journal of Psychology*, *38*, 1–17.

Ghamari-Tabrizi, B. (1996). Is Islamic science possible? *Social Epistemology*
(Special issue: Islamic Social Epistemology), *10*, 317–330. doi:10.1080/
02691729608578822

Gibbons, J. L., & Carr, S. C. (2016). IPP–Quo vadis? *International
Perspectives in Psychology: Research, Practice, Consultation*, *5*, 207–210.
doi:10.1037/ipp0000062

Goonatilake, S. (1998). *Toward a global science: Mining civilizational knowledge*. Bloomington: Indiana University Press.

Guba, E. G., & Lincoln, Y. S. (1994). Competing paradigms in qualitative research. In N. K. Denzin & Y. S. Lincoln (Eds.), *Handbook of qualitative research* (pp. 105–117). Thousand Oaks: Sage.

Hadjistavropoulos, T. (2009). Presidential Address: Canadian psychology in a global context. *Canadian Psychology, 50,* 1–7. doi:10.1037/a0013398

Hemlin, S., Allwood, C. M., & Martin, B. R. (2008). Creative knowledge environments. *Creativity Research Journal, 20,* 196–210. doi:10.1080/10400410802060018

Hemlin, S., Allwood, C. M., Martin, B., & Mumford, M. M. (2013a). *Introduction: Why is leadership important for creativity in science, technology and innovation?* In S. Hemlin, C. M. Allwood, B. Martin, & M. M. Mumford (Eds.), *Creativity and leadership in science technology and innovation* (pp. 1–26). New York: Routledge.

Hemlin, S., Allwood, C. M., Martin, B., & Mumford, M. M. (2013b). Conclusion. In S. Hemlin, C. M. Allwood, B. Martin, & M. M. Mumford (Eds.), *Creativity and leadership in science technology and innovation* (pp. 316–331). New York: Routledge.

Henrich, J., Heine, S., & Norenzayan, A. (2010). The WEIRDest people in the world? *Behavioral and Brain Sciences, 33,* 61–135. doi:10.1017/S0140525X0999152X

Ho, D. Y. F. (1998). Indigenous psychologies: Asian perspectives. *Journal of Cross-Cultural Psychology, 29,* 88–103. doi:10.1177/0022022198291005

Huff, T. E. (1996). Can scientific knowledge be Islamized? *Social Epistemology* (Special issue: *Islamic Social Epistemology*), *10,* 305–316. doi:10.1080/02691729608578821

Hwang, K.-K. (2005). From anti-colonialism to postcolonialism: The emergence of Chinese indigenous psychology in Taiwan. *International Journal of Psychology, 40,* 228–238. doi:10.1080/00207590444000177

Hwang, K.-K. (2006). Constructive realism and Confucian relationalism: An epistemological strategy for the development of indigenous psychology. In U. Kim, K.-S. Yang, & K.-K. Hwang (Eds.), *Indigenous and cultural psychology: Understanding people in context* (pp. 73–107). New York: Springer.

Hwang, K.-K. (2011a). Reification of culture in indigenous psychologies: Merit or mistake? *Social Epistemology, 25,* 125–131. doi:10.1080/02691728.2011.552125

Hwang, K.-K. (2011b). The implication of Popper's anti-inductive theory for the development of indigenous psychologies. *Psychological Studies*, *55*, 390–394. doi:10.1007/s12646-010-0050-1

Hwang, K.-K. (2013a). Indigenous psychology. In K. D. Keith (Ed.), *The encyclopedia of cross-cultural psychology: Vol. 2* (pp. 716–718). Chichester: Wiley-Blackwell. doi:10.1002/9781118339893.wbeccp025

Hwang, K.-K. (2013b). The construction of culture-inclusive theories by multiple philosophical paradigms. *Social Epistemology Review and Reply Collective*, *2*(7), 46–58. http://wp.me/p1Bfg0-PL

Hwang, K.-K. (2015). Cultural system vs pan-cultural dimensions: Philosophical reflection on approaches for indigenous psychology. *Journal for the Theory of Social Behaviour*, *45*, 2–25. doi:10.1111/jtsb.12051

Inayatullah, S. (1996). Islamic responses to emerging scientific, technological and epistemological transformations. *Social Epistemology* (Special issue: Islamic Social Epistemology), *10*, 331–349. doi:10.1080/02691729608578823

Jahoda, G. (2016). On the rise and decline of "indigenous psychology." *Culture & Psychology*, *22*, 169–181. doi:10.1177/1354067X16634052

Jing, Q., & Fu, X. (2001). Modern Chinese psychology: Its indigenous roots and international influences. *International Journal of Psychology*, *36*, 408–418. doi:10.1080/00207590143000234

Kao, H. S. R., & Sinha, D. (Eds.). (1997). *Asian perspectives on psychology* (Vol. 19, Cross-cultural research and methodology series). London: Sage Publications.

Kashima, Y. (2005). Is culture a problem for social psychology? *Asian Journal of Social Psychology*, *8*, 19–38. doi:10.1111/j.1467-839X.2005.00154.x

Kim, U. (1995). Psychology, science, and culture: Cross-cultural analysis of national psychologies. *International Journal of Psychology*, *30*, 663–679. doi:10.1080/00207599508246593

Kim, U., & Berry, J. W. (1993a). Introduction. In U. Kim & J. W. Berry (Eds.), *Indigenous psychologies: Research and experience in cultural context* (pp. 1–29). Newbury Park: Sage.

Kim, U., & Berry, J. W. (Eds.). (1993b). *Indigenous psychologies: Research and experience in cultural context*. Newbury Park: Sage.

Kim, U., Park, Y.-S., & Park, D. (1999). The Korean indigenous psychology approach: Theoretical considerations and empirical applications. *Applied Psychology: An International Review*, *48*, 451–464. doi:10.1111/j.1464-0597.1999.tb00065.x

Kim, U., Park, Y.-S., & Park, D. (2000). The challenge of cross-cultural psychology: The role of the indigenous psychologies. *Journal of Cross-Cultural Psychology, 31*, 63–75. doi:10.1177/0022022100031001006

Kim, U., & Park, Y.-S. (2005). Integrated analysis of indigenous psychologies: Comments and extensions of ideas presented by Shams, Jackson, Hwang and Kashima. *Asian Journal of Social Psychology, 8*, 75–95. doi:10.1111/j.1467-839X.2005.00162.x

Kim, U., & Park, Y.-S. (2006). The scientific foundation of indigenous and cultural psychology: The transactional approach. In U. Kim, K.-S. Yang, & K.-K. Hwang (Eds.), *Indigenous and cultural psychology: Understanding people in context* (pp. 27–48). New York: Springer.

Kim, U., Yang, K.-S., & Hwang, K.-K. (Eds). (2006a). *Indigenous and cultural psychology: Understanding people in context.* New York: Springer.

Kim, U., Yang, K.-S. & Hwang, K.-K. (2006b). Contributions to indigenous and cultural psychology: Understanding people in context. In U. Kim, K.-S. Yang, & K.-K. Hwang (Eds.), *Indigenous and cultural psychology: Understanding people in context* (pp. 3–25). New York: Springer.

Leung, K., & Zhang, J. (1995). Systemic considerations: Factors facilitating and impeding the development of psychology in developing countries. *International Journal of Psychology* (Special issue: National development of psychology: Factors facilitating and impeding progress in developing countries), *30*, 693–706. doi:10.1080/00207599508246595

Liu, J. H. (2011). On the limited foundations of western skepticism towards indigenous psychological thinking: Pragmatics, politics, and philosophy of indigenous psychology. *Social Epistemology, 25*, 133–140. doi:10.1080/02691728.2011.552126

Llewellyn, J. E. (Ed.). (2005). *Defining Hinduism: A reader.* London: Equinox Publishing.

Long, W. (2014). Critical reflections on the Islamicisation of psychology. *Revelation and Science, 4*(1), 14–19.

Lonner, W. J. (2013). Foreword. In K. D. Keith (Ed.), *The encyclopedia of cross-cultural psychology: Vol. 1* (pp. xl–xlx). Chichester: Wiley-Blackwell. doi:10.1002/9781118339893.wbeccp025

Mate-Kole. C. C. (2013). Psychology in Ghana revisited. *Journal of Black Psychology, 39*, 316–320. doi:10.1177/0095798413480664

Maxwell, J. A. (2004a). Causal explanation, qualitative research, and scientific inquiry in education. *Educational Research, 33*, 3–11. doi:10.3102/0013189X033002003

Maxwell, J. A. (2004b). Using qualitative methods for causal explanation. *Field Methods, 16*, 243–264. doi:10.1177/1525822X04266831

Mayer, S. (2002). Psychology in Nigeria: a view from the outside. *Ife PsychologIA An International Journal*, *10*, 1–8. doi:10.4314/ifep.v10i1.23481

McCrae, R. R., & Terracciano, A. (2006). National character and personality. *Current Directions in Psychological Science*, *15*, 156–161. doi:10.1111/j. 1467-8721.2006.00427.x

Misra, G. (1998). Obituary: Professor Durganand Sinha (1922–1998). Cross-Cultural Psychology Bulletin, September, 6–10.

Misra, G., Jain, U., & Singh, T. (2002). Culture and social cognition: The Indian experience. In G. Misra & A. K. Mohanty (Eds.), *Perspectives on indigenous psychology* (pp. 224–248). New Dehli: Concept Publishing Company.

Misra, G., & Mohanty, A. K. (Eds.). (2002), *Perspectives on indigenous psychology*. New Delhi: Concept Publishing Company.

Misra, G., & Paranjpe, A. C. (2012). Psychology in modern India. In R. W. Rieber (Ed.), *Encyclopedia of the history of psychological theories* (Part 16; pp. 881–892). New York: Springer.

Moghaddam, F. M., & Taylor, D. M. (1985). Psychology in the developing world: An evaluation through the concepts of "dual perception" and "parallel growth." *American Psychologist*, *40*, 1144–1146. doi:10.1037/0003-066X.40.10.1144

Morris, M. W., Chiu, C., & Liu, Z. (2015). Polycultural psychology. *Annual Review of Psychology*, *66*, 631–659. doi:10.1146/annurev-psych-010814-015001

Mullainathan, S. & Shafir, E. (2013). *Scarcity The true cost of not having enough*. London, UK: Penguin.

Norenzayan, A. (2013). *Big gods: How religion transformed cooperation and conflict*. Princeton: Princeton University Press.

Nikora, L. W. (2007). Māori and psychology: Indigenous psychology in New Zealand. In A. Weatherall, M. Wilson, D. Harper, & J. McDowall (Eds.), *Psychology in Aotearoa/New Zealand* (pp. 80–85). Auckland: Pearson Education New Zealand.

Nisbett, R. E. (2003). *The geography of thought: How Asians and Westerners think differently . . . and why*. New York: The Free Press.

Nisbett, R. E., & Ross, L. (1980). *Human inference: Strategies and short-comings of social judgment*. Englewood Cliffs: Prentice-Hall.

Nisbett, R. E., & Wilson, T. D. (1977). Telling more than we can know: Verbal reports on mental processes. *Psychological Review*, *84*, 231–259. doi:10.1037/0033-295X.84.3.231

Nsamenang, A. B. (2013). Cameroon black psychologists. *Journal of Black Psychology*, *39*, 307–310. doi:10.1177/0095798413480662

Ojalehto, B. L. & Medin, D. L. (2015). Perspectives on culture and concepts. *Annual Review of Psychology*, *66*, 249–275. doi:10.1146/annurev-psych-010814-015120

Open Science Collaboration (2015). Estimating the reproducibility of psychological science. *Science*, 349 (6251), aac4716. doi:10.1126/science.aac4716

Oppong, S. (2016). The journey towards Africanising psychology in Ghana. *Psychological Thought*, *9*, 1–14. doi:10.5964/psyct.v9i1.128

Padalia, D. (2017). Why indigenous psychology? A review article. *The International Journal of Indian Psychology*, *4*, 78–82. doi:10.25215/0403.151

Pandey, J. (1998). Obituary: Professor Durganand Sinha (1922–1998). *Journal of Cross-Cultural Psychology*, *29*, 691–694. doi:10.1177/0022022198296001

Pe-Pua, R. (2015). Indigenous psychology. In J. D. Wright (Ed.), *International encyclopedia of the social & behavioural sciences* (2nd edn.; pp. 788–794). Oxford: Elsevier.

Pe-Pua, R., & Protacio-Marcelino, E. (2000). Sikolohiyang Pilipino (Filipino psychology): A legacy to Virgilio Enriquez. *Asian Journal of Social Psychology*, *3*, 49–71. doi:10.1111/1467-839X.00054

Poortinga, Y. H. (1999). Do differences in behaviour imply a need for different psychologies? *Applied Psychology: An International Review*, *48*, 419–432. doi:10.1080/026999499377394

Poortinga, Y. H. (2016). Integration of basic controversies in cross-cultural psychology. *Psychology & Developing Societies*, *28*, 161–182. doi:10.1177/0971333616657169

Raina, D. (1997). Evolving perspectives on science and history: A chronicle of modern India's scientific enchantment and disenchantment. *Social Epistemology*, *11*, 3–24. doi:10.1080/02691729708578826

Randerson, A. K. (2015). Human sensitivity towards nature: Eastern and Western perspectives. *World Journal of Science, Technology and Sustainable Development*, *12*(3), 172–182. doi:10.1108/WJSTSD-05-2015-0023

Saberwal, S. (1982). Uncertain transplants: Anthropology and sociology in India. *Ethnos*, *47*, 36–49. doi:10.1080/00141844.1982.9981230

San Juan, Jr, E. (2006). Toward a decolonizing indigenous psychology in the Philippines: Introducing Sikolohiyang Pilipino. *Journal for Cultural Research*, *10*, 47–67. doi:10.1080/14797580500422018

Sanzez Sosa, J. J., & Valderrama-Iturbe, P. (2001). Psychology in Latin America: Historical reflections and perspectives. *International Journal of Psychology*, *36*, 384–394. doi:10.1080/00207590143000216

Shadish, W. R., Cook, T. D., & Campbell, D. T. (2002). *Experimental and quasi-experimental design for generalized causal inference*. Boston: Houghton Mifflin Company.

Shams, M. (2002). Issues in the study of Indigenous psychologies: Historical perspectives, cultural interdependence and institutional regulations. *Asian Journal of Social Psychology, 5*, 79–91. doi:10.1111/1467-839X.00096

Shams, M. (2005). Developmental issues in indigenous psychologies: sustainability and local knowledge. *Asian Journal of Social Psychology, 8*, 39–50. doi:10.1111/j.1467-839X.2005.00155.x

Sharma, D. (2015). Durganand Sinha: The pioneering work of an Indian psychologist. In G. J. Rich & U. P. Gielen (Eds.), *Pathfinders in international psychology* (pp. 187–199). Charlotte: Information Age Publishing.

Shiraev, E., & Levy, D. (2013). National character. In K. D. Keith (Ed.), *The encyclopedia of cross-cultural psychology*: Vol. 2 (pp. 917–919). Chichester: Wiley-Blackwell. doi:10.1002/9781118339893.wbeccp025

Shweder, R. (1990). Cultural psychology –What is it? In J. Stigler, R. Shweder, & G. Herdt (Eds.), *Cultural psychology: Essays on comparative human development* (pp. 1–43). New York: Cambridge University Press.

Shweder, R. (2000). The psychology of practice and the practice of three psychologies. *Asian Journal of Social Psychology, 3*, 207–222. doi:10.1111/1467-839X.00065

Sinha, D. (1986). *Psychology in a third world country*. New Delhi: Sage.

Sinha, D. (1993). Indigenization of psychology in India and its relevance. In U. Kim & J. W. Berry (Eds.), *Indigenous psychologies: Research and experience in cultural context* (pp. 30–43). Newbury Park: Sage.

Sinha, D. (1997). Indigenizing psychology. In J. W. Berry, Y. H. Poortinga, & J. Pandey (Eds.), *Handbook of cross-cultural psychology: Vol. 1. Theory and method* (pp. 129–169). Boston: Allyn & Bacon.

Sinha, D. (2002). Culture and psychology: Perspective of cross-cultural psychology. *Psychology and Developing Societies, 14*, 11–25. doi:10.1177/097133360201400102

Sinha, D., & Sinha, M. (1997). Orientations to psychology: Asian and Western. In H. S. R. Kao & D. Sinha (Eds.), *Asian perspectives on psychology* (Vol. 19: Cross-cultural research and methodology series; pp. 25–39). London: Sage Publications.

Sinha, D., & Tripathi, R. C. (1994). Individualism in a collectivist culture: A case of coexistence of opposites. In U. Kim, H. C. Triandis, C. Kâğitçibaşi, S.-C. Choi & G. Yoon (Eds), *Individualism and collectivism: Theory, method, and applications* (pp. 123–136). Thousand Oaks: SAGE Publications.

Sinha, J. B. P. (1995). Factors facilitating and impeding growth of psychology in South Asia with special reference to India. *International Journal of Psychology* (Special issue: National development of psychology: Factors facilitating and impeding progress in developing countries), *30*, 741–753.

Sismondo, S. (2004). *An introduction to science and technology studies.* Malden: Blackwell.

Smith, P. B. (2010). On the distinctiveness of Chinese psychology; or: Are we all Chinese? In M. H. Bond (Ed.), *Oxford handbook of Chinese psychology* (pp. 699–710). New York: Oxford University Press.

Stringer, H. (2018). The healing power of heritage. *Monitor on Psychology, 49* (2), 44–51.

Sundararajan, L., Kim, U., & Park, Y.-S. (2017). Indigenous psychologies. In J. Stein (Ed.), *Reference module in neuroscience and biobehavioral psychology* (pp. 1–7). Amsterdam: Elsevier.

Sundararajan, L., Misra, G., & Marsella, A. J. (2013). Indigenous approaches to assessment, diagnosis, and treatment of mental disorders. In F. A. Paniagua & A.-M. Yamada (Eds.), *Handbook of multicultural mental health* (pp. 69–88). Oxford: Academic Press.

Sulayman, A. (1989). *Islamization of knowledge: General principles and a workplan* (2nd edn.). Herndon: International Institute of Islamic Thought.

Terracciano, A., Abdel-Khalek, A. M., Ádám, N., Adamovová, L., Ahn, C.-K., Ahn, H.-N.,... McCrae, R. R. (2005). National character does not reflect mean personality trait levels in 49 cultures. *Science, 310*(5745), 96–100. doi:10.1126/science.1117199

Thorngate, W. (2008, March). Psychology in Iran. *Observer* (Association for Psychological Science), 21(3) www.psychologicalscience.org/observer/psy chology-in-iran

Tohidi, N. (2016). Women's rights and feminist movements in Iran. *SUR International Journal on Human Rights, 13*, 75–89.

Torres, H., & Consoli, A. (June, 2015). Moving towards a new relationship with Latin American psychology. *Psychology International, 26*(2), 5–8.

Tuck, E. (2013). Commentary: Decolonizing methodologies 15 years later. *AlterNative: An International Journal of Indigenous Peoples, 9*, 365–72. doi:10.1177/117718011300900407

Wagner, W., Duveen, G., Themel, M., & Verma, J. (1999). The modernization of tradition: Thinking about madness in Patna, India. *Culture & Psychology, 5*, 413–445. doi:10.1177/1354067X9954003

Weber, E. U., & Morris, M. W. (2010). Culture and judgment and decision making: The constructivist turn. *Perspectives on Psychological Science, 5*, 410–419. doi:10.1177/1745691610375556

Yang, K.-S. (1997). Indigenising Westernized Chinese psychology. In M.H. Bond (Ed.), *Working at the interface of culture: Eighteen lives in social science* (pp. 62–76). London: Routledge.

Yang, K.-S. (2012). Indigenous psychology, Westernized psychology, and indigenized psychology: A non-Western psychologist's view. *Chang Gung Journal of Humanities and Social Sciences*, 5(1), 1–32.

Yearley, S. (2005). *Making sense of science*. London: Sage Publications.

Ziman, J. (2000). *Real science: What it is, and what it means*. Cambridge: Cambridge University Press.

Cambridge Elements ≡

Psychology and Culture

Kenneth D. Keith

University of San Diego

Kenneth D. Keith is author or editor of more than 160 publications on cross-cultural psychology, quality of life, intellectual disability, and the teaching of psychology. He was the 2017 president of the Society for the Teaching of Psychology.

About the series

Elements in Psychology and Culture features authoritative surveys and updates on key topics in cultural, cross-cultural, and indigenous psychology. Authors are internationally recognized scholars whose work is at the forefront of their subdisciplines within the realm of psychology and culture.

Cambridge Elements ☰

Psychology and Culture

Elements in the series

The Continuing Growth of Cross-Cultural Psychology: A First-Person Annotated Chronology
Walter J. Lonner

Measuring and Interpreting Subjective Wellbeing in Different Cultural Contexts: A Review and Way Forward
Robert A. Cummins

The Nature and Challenges of Indigenous Psychologies
Carl Martin Allwood

A full series listing is available at: www.cambridge.org/EPAC

Printed in the United States
By Bookmasters